THE
ACCIDENTAL
CREATIVE

THE ACCIDENTAL CREATIVE

HOW TO BE BRILLIANT AT A MOMENT'S NOTICE

TODD HENRY

PORTFOLIO / PENGUIN

PORTFOLIO / PENGUIN
Published by the Penguin Group
Penguin Group (USA) Inc., 375 Hudson Street,
New York, New York 10014, U.S.A.
Penguin Group (Canada), 90 Eglinton Avenue East, Suite 700,
Toronto, Ontario, Canada M4P 2Y3
(a division of Pearson Penguin Canada Inc.)
Penguin Books Ltd, 80 Strand, London WC2R 0RL, England
Penguin Ireland, 25 St. Stephen's Green, Dublin 2, Ireland
(a division of Penguin Books Ltd)
Penguin Books Australia Ltd, 250 Camberwell Road, Camberwell,
Victoria 3124, Australia
(a division of Pearson Australia Group Pty Ltd)
Penguin Books India Pvt Ltd, 11 Community Centre, Panchsheel Park,
New Delhi – 110 017, India
Penguin Group (NZ), 67 Apollo Drive, Rosedale, Auckland 0632,
New Zealand (a division of Pearson New Zealand Ltd)
Penguin Books (South Africa) (Pty) Ltd, 24 Sturdee Avenue,
Rosebank, Johannesburg 2196, South Africa

Penguin Books Ltd, Registered Offices:
80 Strand, London WC2R 0RL, England

First published in 2011 by Portfolio / Penguin,
a member of Penguin Group (USA) Inc.

10   9   8   7   6   5   4   3   2   1

LIBRARY OF CONGRESS CATALOGING IN PUBLICATION DATA

Henry, Todd.
    The accidental creative : how to be brilliant at a moment's notice / Todd Henry.
       p. cm.
    Includes index.
    ISBN 978-1-59184-401-3
    1. Creative ability in business.   2. Critical thinking.   3. Teams in the workplace.   4. Success in business.
I. Title.
    HD53.H46 2011
    650.1—dc22

                                                                                2011002127

Printed in the United States of America
Set in ITC New Baskerville Std
Designed by Pauline Neuwirth, Neuwirth & Associates

To Ethan, Owen, and Ava, who regularly show me what creativity
is all about, and to Rachel for the freedom.
I love you all.

CONTENTS

THE
ACCIDENTAL
CREATIVE

THE ACCIDENTAL CREATIVE

In some circles, the word "creative" has recently morphed from adjective to noun. If you are one of the millions among us who make a living with your mind, you could be tagged a "creative." Every day, you solve problems, innovate, develop systems, design things, write, think, and strategize. You are responsible for moving big conceptual rocks, crafting systems that form the foundations for future growth—creating value that didn't exist before you arrived on the scene.

Maybe you didn't set out to be a creative. In fact, perhaps you even cringe when you hear the word applied to you. Understandably, the tag "creative" sometimes conjures up images of SoHo advertising gurus flitting about in five-hundred-dollar designer jeans. You may prefer the term "strategist" or "manager," or something else that feels more *concrete*. Call yourself anything you want, but if you're responsible for solving problems, developing strategies, or otherwise straining your brain for new ideas, I'm going to call you a creative—even if you ended up being one accidentally.

Some people deliberately choose a career that allows them to exercise their creativity on a daily basis. They make their livings designing, writing, developing ad campaigns, or doing some other kind of conceptual work. They get to do something they love, and someone gives them money for it. Speaking as one of the last group, I think it's a pretty great deal. On our best days it seems almost unfair that we get paid to do what we do, but on our worst days our jobs feel pretty much like any other. Though creative fields may sound exotic to strangers at cocktail parties, our day-to-day work can often feel a lot like following recipes, taking familiar ingredients and mixing them together in slightly different ways.

Whichever type you are, creative or "accidental creative," this book will help you create faster and more effectively than you ever imagined possible.

For the traditional creatives, such as designers, writers, visual artists, musicians, and performers, this book will help you establish enough structure in your life to get the most out of your creative process. It will also teach you how to stay engaged and prolific over the long term, which is often a problem for artists who must produce continually on demand.

For the nontraditional creatives, such as managers, strategists, consultants, salespeople, and client service reps, this book will help you unlock your latent creative abilities. You will learn how to do what many brilliant creatives already do instinctively, and how to do it consistently. In short, you will learn how to be brilliant when it counts the most.

There are tremendous benefits to doing creative work. You get to add unique value, carve out your own niche in the marketplace, and watch your notions and hunches go from conception to execution; could there be any type of work more gratifying? But the flip side of this is that whether you are a designer, manager, writer, consultant, or programmer, you are required to create value each and every day without reprieve. The work never ends, and as long as there is "just one more thing" to think about, finding time to rest can be difficult. Your primary tool, your mind, goes with you everywhere. If your job is to solve problems—to create—then you are always looking for new ideas. In addition, you won't always have the option of going back to your desk to quietly brainstorm, vetting your ideas one by one. As a creative, you will regularly find yourself in situations that require you to generate brilliant ideas at a moment's notice.

This is no easy feat. If you want to deliver the right idea at the right moment, you must begin the process far upstream from when you need that idea. You need to build practices into your life that will help you focus your creative energy. There is a persistent myth in the workplace that creativity is a mystical and elusive force that sits somewhere between prayer and the U.S. tax code on the ambiguity scale. But the reality is that you can unquestionably increase your capacity to experience regular flashes of creative insight—"creative accidents"—bring the best of who you are to your work, and execute more effectively, all by building purposeful practices into your life to help you do so. These practices will help you stay engaged and productive over the long term without experiencing the rampant burnout that often plagues creative workers.

In other words, purposeful preparation and training using the tools in this book will directly increase your capacity to do brilliant work, day after day, year after year.

> **If you want to deliver the right idea at the right moment, you must begin the process far upstream from when you need that idea.**

Why am I so sure it works? I've spent years working with traditionally "creative" workers (designers, writers, musicians, filmmakers) and traditionally "noncreative" workers (salespeople, real estate agents, accountants), helping them develop their creative strength and stamina. In addition to this work with my company, Accidental Creative, and my experience as a leader of creative teams, I've also conducted countless interviews with creative thinkers, productivity experts, and organizational leaders, such as David Allen (*Getting Things Done*); Seth Godin (*Linchpin, Tribes, Purple Cow*); riCardo Crespo (Senior Vice President, Global Creative Chief, Twentieth Century Fox FCP); Richard Westendorf (Executive Creative Director, Landor Associates); Scott Belsky (CEO of Behance and author of *Making Ideas Happen*); Tony Schwartz (*The Way We're Working Isn't Working, The Power of Full Engagement*); and Keith Ferrazzi (*Never Eat Alone, Who's Got Your Back*); among others.

Astonishingly, I've found little difference among the pressures experienced by these diverse groups of people. They each use a different set of specific skills in their work, of course. While a designer will solve a problem visually, a manager may solve it by developing a new process. But they're both employing the same creative tools and wrestling with many of the same obstacles. The good news is that, regardless of role, you can improve your ability to generate good ideas consistently if you are willing to be a little more purposeful in how you approach the creative process. It won't be easy, but in the end your work will be more satisfying, more productive, and more fun.

HOW TO READ THIS BOOK

This book is divided into two sections. Chapters 1 through 3 deal with many of the pressures faced by creatives in the workplace, and why doing brilliant work day after day can be so challenging. Chapters 4 through 10 offer some practices that you can implement to help you experience higher levels of creative insight on a daily basis. While you may be tempted to skip ahead to the latter portion of the book, I would recommend that you begin with the first chapters. Some dynamics that affect the everyday experiences of the creative are painfully felt but are seldom diagnosed, and can have a dramatic effect on your ability to do your best work.

> **Anyone can improve his ability to generate good ideas consistently if willing to be a little more purposeful in how to approach the creative process.**

Before you dive in, however, there are a few critical ideas to digest:

It's not what you know that matters, it's what you do. Regardless of what others may promise, there are no quick fixes or easy steps to supercharge your creativity. You will unleash your latent creative ability through regular, purposeful practice of the principles in this book. There are most certainly insights and "aha!" moments to be found in these pages, but knowledge alone won't do the job any more than knowing the fundamentals of how to exercise will keep you physically healthy. You must be purposeful and intentional. The results are worth it.

You own your growth. Regardless of your circumstances, you are the ultimate owner of your own creative growth. It's not your manager's responsibility, or your HR director's, or your mother's—it's yours. Many people waste years of their life pointing fingers at other people for their own problems. No doubt there are some very unhealthy organizations and managers out there, but at the end of the day, playing the victim is a loser's game. Own your growth.

It's going to take time, and short-term results may vary. As with anything worthwhile, restructuring your life to work in concert with the dynamics of the creative process will take time and dedication. In addition, there will always be circumstances beyond your control that affect your engagement from time to time. Because of this, the results of implementing these practices may vary during a specific period. Your eye should be on increased performance over time, not on snapshot productivity. Don't lose heart. Stay engaged.

This is about more than just your work life. It's more and more difficult in today's world to segment your life into buckets like "work," "home," "relationships," "hobbies," and so on. Every area of your life affects every other, and a lack of engagement in one area will quickly infect the rest. As you implement these practices, you will find that your newfound creative energy will infiltrate not just your work life, but all other areas of your life as well. A rising tide raises all boats.

I believe that your best work is ahead of you. Remember: No one lies on his deathbed wishing he'd had the time to reply to one more e-mail, but a great many people express regrets about not having treated life with more purpose. By applying the principles and practices in this book, you will be poised to get moving on things that previously seemed unattainable.

Now let's get started.

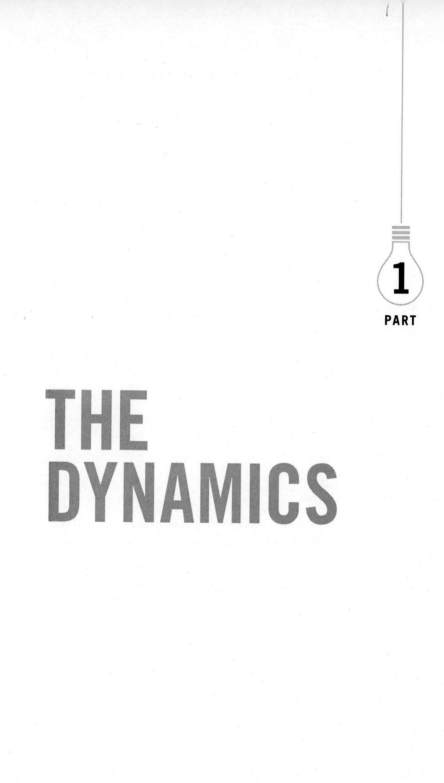

THE
DYNAMICS

THE DYNAMICS
OF CREATIVE WORK

1.

Creative work comes with a unique set of pressures.
We're compensated for the ideas we generate, the value we create, and the problems we solve, and though we may be good at what we do, many of us may feel at least a little out of touch with the mysterious process by which any of this happens. On some days, ideas spring forth effortlessly, and we feel poised to attack any problem that comes our way. On others, we struggle with a single obstacle without any significant momentum. It can be frustrating to be held responsible for something we have so little control over, especially in the marketplace, where our career success is directly tied to our ability to generate great ideas consistently.

Many of us assume that our creative process is beyond our ability to influence, and we pay attention to it only when it isn't working properly. For the most part, we go about our daily tasks and everything just "works." Until it doesn't. We treat our creative process like a household appliance. It's just expected to work quietly in the background, and we lose sight of how much we depend on it until the day we're stuck with dirty socks.

Adding to this lack of understanding is the rapidly accelerating pace of work. Each day we are faced with escalating expectations and a continual squeeze to do more with less. We are asked to produce ever-increasing amounts of brilliance in ever-shrinking amounts of time. There is an unspoken (or spoken!) expectation that we'll be accessible 24/7, and as a result we frequently feel like we're "always on." And because each new project starts with a blank slate, we feel like we have to prove ourselves again and again. No matter how successful we've been in the past, each new project elicits the question: "Do I still have it in me?"

LIFE IN THE "CREATE ON DEMAND" WORLD

A few years ago my company, Accidental Creative, coined a term to describe this workplace dynamic: "create on demand." You go to work each day tasked with (1) inventing brilliant solutions that (2) meet specific objectives by (3) defined deadlines. If you do this successfully you get to keep your job. If you don't, you get to work on your résumé. The moment you exchange your creative efforts for money, you enter a world where you will have to be brilliant at a moment's notice. (No pressure, right?)

No matter whether you are leading a team, developing marketing strategies, running a small business, or writing copy, when you are compensated for creating value with your mind, the pressure to perform is palpable. Because brilliant ideas seem to be a free and renewable resource, it's easy for you (and your boss) to believe that you can incrementally ratchet up your productivity without experiencing side effects. But this understanding of the economics of creating is not only false, it can also be damaging both to your ability to do your best work now and to your long-term sustainability as a creative. To attempt to be perpetually brilliant and increasingly productive, without changing the basic habits and structure of your life to accommodate that undertaking, is a futile effort.

The always-on manner with which many creatives approach their work is arrhythmic, but the creative process is naturally rhythmic. There are peaks and troughs of productivity, an ebb and flow to idea generation. Working harder and staring more intently at the problem to achieve better ideas is like trying to control the weather by staring at the clouds. Rather, you need to incorporate practices that instill a sense of structure, rhythm, and purpose into your life. You need to create space for your creative process to thrive rather than expect it to operate in the cracks of your frenetic schedule. This will not only help you generate better ideas now, but it will also ensure that you are acting on the things that matter most instead of drifting through your days.

Many young creatives I've worked with have looked at me skeptically, and even angrily, when I talk about being more purposeful about where they spend their time and energy. To them, creativity flows freely from a spigot; they can work fifteen-hour days with little reprieve and no apparent side effects. But eventually this kind of behavior catches up to you. When you violate the natural rhythms of the creative process, you may initially produce a very high volume of work, but you will eventually find that you're not producing your best work. Instead, you may find that you are trending toward mediocrity, and that great ideas are no longer coming with the frequency you'd prefer. This is a very unsatisfying way to live and to work, and feels a lot more like surviving than thriving.

> **To attempt to be perpetually brilliant and increasingly productive, without changing the basic habits and structure of your life to accommodate that undertaking, is a futile effort.**

This book is about learning to *thrive* in the create-on-demand world. To do so will require you to make some real changes to the way you structure your life, and the way you think about what you do. Your best creative work will follow.

BEING SUSTAINABLY BRILLIANT

Whenever someone asks me what I do, I like to say that I'm an "arms dealer for the creative revolution." My job is to equip creatives for the pressures and demands of the marketplace by providing them with the tools they need to experience consistent brilliance in their life and work. Because of this, whenever I speak to a group of creatives at a company or conference, or sit with anyone one-on-one in a coaching session, I challenge them to adopt the goal of being prolific, brilliant, and healthy:

Prolific + Brilliant + Healthy = producing great work
consistently and in a sustainable way

This is the most effective way to live and work. It means producing a large volume of high-quality work over long periods of time. In my experience, most creatives consistently perform very well in two of these areas, but are lacking at least one of them. For instance,

Prolific + Brilliant − Healthy = Burnout

While the overstressed, "gasping for air" worker is the celebrated hero of office folklore, for the creative, being one of these is simply not a realistic and sustainable way to do great work. Many creatives sacrifice their long-term viability on the altar of short-term productivity; they eventually discover that the trade-off simply isn't worth it. They find that they can no longer sustain their pace and that their ideas—which were once plentiful and brilliant—have dried up. The common term for this is "burn-out," and unfortunately, it doesn't just affect our work. Creatives who struggle with burnout find it infiltrating their home life, relationships, and personal projects as well. Not good.

Hard work is an absolute necessity if you want to do anything worthwhile. In fact, if you apply the principles in this book, you will probably end up working harder than you ever have in your entire career. But what you must avoid is the kind of frenetic activity that seems like productivity but is really more about the appearance of being busy than the actual accomplishment of effective work. You want to work strategically, not desperately. When it comes to your effectiveness, fake work is often more dangerous than no work at all.

Brilliant + Healthy – Prolific = Unreliable

The create-on-demand world requires that you produce results consistently. While there are a few untouchable genius creatives who are capable of cranking out only a few new projects per year—and then are paid tons of money for their efforts—most creatives are required to produce consistently if they want to keep their jobs. This means that you need to have great ideas and execute them consistently in order to meet expectations.

> **When it comes to your effectiveness, fake work is often more dangerous than no work at all.**

Similarly, many creatives have a lot of great ideas but are ineffective at execution. They never "ship" because they are too busy obsessively perfecting and tweaking their ideas. To be prolific means that you not only have great ideas, but that you actually do something with them. You can't be bound by insecurity and neurosis. You must ship if you want to thrive.

Healthy + Prolific – Brilliant = Fired

At one point or another you've probably worked with someone who just couldn't keep pace with everyone else in the office. You don't want to be that person. With the ever-increasing competition in the workplace, creatives who keep their jobs and get promoted are the ones who can separate themselves from the pack. Mediocrity is unacceptable and will not be tolerated for long in most good organizations. Brilliance, on the other hand, is about rising to the occasion, seeing clearly and incisively to the core of the problem, and identifying great solutions quickly. If you apply the practices in the later chapters of this book, you can consistently experience this kind of brilliance in your work.

So where do you fall in this equation? Would you describe yourself as all three—prolific, brilliant, and healthy? Or is there room for improvement in one or more areas? If you find that you're doing pretty well on two of the three, don't worry, you're not alone. I rarely meet creatives or teams that are firing on all cylinders. With the complexities and shifting landscape of many workplaces, just to stay ahead of the work is often challenging enough.

CAN CREATIVITY TRULY BE INFLUENCED?

When I consider the confusion that surrounds the creative process, I'm reminded of an insight I had while sick as a dog on the living-room couch. Home from work and bored silly, I decided to see what was on TV at two o'clock on a Wednesday afternoon. (If you've never tried it, prepare for disappointment.) Eventually, I landed on PBS, where I was immediately entranced by the persona of Dr. Julius Sumner Miller, host of *Demonstrations in Physics*. Dr. Miller wielded a plank of wood in one hand and a newspaper in the other. He placed the plank on a table in front of him with about a third of it protruding off the edge. He laid the newspaper carefully over the part of the plank resting on the table. Glaring intensely into the camera, he asked, "What do you think will happen when I strike the protruding end of this plank of wood?"

Having a basic understanding of how levers work, I deduced that the edge of the table would act as a fulcrum and that the plank would flip the newspaper into the air and, if I was lucky, provide some comic relief as the plank broke a flask or two on the table behind Dr. Miller. (Maybe my afternoon could be salvaged after all!)

Imagine my surprise when Dr. Miller's hand snapped the plank in two! How could this be? It made no sense. The newspaper surely wasn't heavy enough to hold a quarter-inch-thick wooden plank so tightly. There was something else going on here.

Cold forgotten, I sat forward on the couch as Dr. Miller explained the unseen force at work: There were close to fifteen pounds of atmospheric pressure pushing down on every square inch of the newspaper. This added up to several thousand pounds of pressure on the paper as a whole. When the plank of wood was struck, as long as there wasn't time for the air pressure to equalize under the paper, this invisible force would hold the plank like a vise as the strike snapped it in half.

I had a sudden insight. I couldn't see atmospheric pressure, so I hadn't been aware of its power prior to this little experiment. I didn't consider its potential influence until Dr. Miller's karate chop showed me how it could be leveraged to accomplish a task—breaking a plank.

I don't think it's much of a stretch to say that many of us view the creative process in the same way. It is a mysterious, unseen force that can have powerful, unanticipated effects. We know it's there, but we don't understand it, and so it seems beyond our ability to control. But like atmospheric pressure, once we grasp a few of its governing dynamics, we can harness its power by building structure to leverage it.

"The enemy of art is the absence of limitations."

—Orson Welles

This suggestion that structure and creativity are two sides of the same coin is often an eyebrow-raiser for my clients. There is the persistent myth that creativity results only from complete lack of boundaries and total freedom. The reality is that we are not capable of operating *without* boundaries. We need them in order to focus our creative energy into the right channels. Total freedom is false freedom. True freedom has healthy boundaries.

I often see in newly minted entrepreneurs the paralysis that results from total freedom. One person I encountered was a highly functioning, brilliantly creative manager in a large company. He had been building his business on the side for quite some time and was somehow able to balance the pressures of his normal 9-to-5 role with the demands of his new venture. At the point he thought it made sense, he struck out on his own and left the corporate world. Finally, he thought, he'd have the capacity to focus full time on his passion for building his business.

But it didn't work that way. Instead, he found that his days lacked structure. He wasn't producing good work. In fact, he wasn't producing much work at all. The highly capable, broad-shouldered manager had vanished, and in his place was a drifting, overwhelmed slacker.

What happened? It wasn't that he was no longer motivated. In fact, he was more motivated than ever. What changed was that the rhythms in his life—many of which were forced by his day job—had disappeared. He no longer had to plan his week according to when he could get work in on his side project, because he had all the time he needed. But time alone isn't sufficient without good structure. Once I was able to work with him to build some simple structure into his week for creating, strategy, and relationships, he found his productivity skyrocketing again. All he lacked was the foundation of rhythm in a few key areas.

You must not confuse structure with formula. They are not the same. A formula is something you apply to get a predictable result on the other side. There is no formula for effective creating. Structure, on the other hand, is the undergirding platform that gives you enough stability to feel free taking risks. It gives you a sense of mastery over your process.

Mastery over your creative process is critical in today's workplace. Unfortunately, when you fall into a pattern of reacting to the everyday pressures of your work, you may unknowingly do things that cause serious damage to your creative muscles. When you feel no control over where and when your next good idea will arrive, you may compensate by working harder and staring more intently at the problem in the hopes that the extra effort will cause brilliance to flow. But this "always on" approach works against you.

AMOS—THE "ACCIDENTAL" CREATIVE

Meet Amos. He is a manager at a Fortune 100 company, and though he's not a typical creative, he faces all the pressures that accompany creative work. Amos is a brilliant, accomplished, and fast-rising leader who is currently helming five major projects for the company. He manages the communication and marketing needs for his department, gleans consumer insights that can be applied to new projects, and coordinates product development input from R&D. In addition, Amos is responsible for developing his direct reports and ensuring that the organization that reports to him is in alignment with the company's priorities. There are several constituencies to please at multiple levels in the organization, and Amos spends a lot of his time just trying to identify his true objectives within the barrage of input he receives from his superiors.

Amos has several meetings over the course of a typical day. Many of these are simple check-ins with his direct reports or with his manager to discuss progress. He may also have longer meetings with his leadership team or with the representatives from the agencies that help his company craft their communications. In addition, Amos manages an insane amount of internal communication, especially e-mail. "It's like a dog trying to swim on a lake," he says, "and the lake is my e-mail. I'm never caught up or able to swim my way out of the lake."

The most difficult thing, according to Amos, is that in the midst of all of the meetings and "pseudo work," he knows that his main job is to "move the needle" and make progress on his projects. He knows that the real value he brings to his company is the ability to generate key ideas at just the right time to properly direct the course of a project. But due to the frenetic schedule he keeps, the constant influx of e-mail, and the pressures of managing the relational expectations, he finds "there is not very much time to actually do work." Amos gets to think about his work much less than he'd like because he's so busy just trying to stay ahead of everything else.

Amos's struggles to gain creative traction are largely the result of pressures he feels in five key areas of work: Focus, Relationships, Energy, Stimuli, and Hours. Let's take a look at how Amos is affected by each of these five areas:

FOCUS

Amos says that gaining Focus can be a real problem in his role. "No one wants to make choices," he explains, "and everyone likes to revisit every decision." As a result, he finds it difficult to know what to focus on at any given time. Old decisions are always open for reanalysis. In addition, Amos says that "work is pushed down, but decisions are pushed up. Thus, it's hard to ever make things move together." For example, critical and timely projects frequently appear on Amos's plate from his manager, but after Amos rearranges his life in order to squeeze the extra work into his schedule, it then takes weeks to push approval of his decisions through to the upper layers of the organization, or he discovers that the scope and priority of the project has changed in the process. To Amos, it seems that objectives are a constantly moving target.

RELATIONSHIPS

To get stuff done, Amos needs buy-in from a herd of stakeholders. As such, there are numerous relationships to manage in order to make progress on his work. This face time takes a toll on him, since much of his real work gets done in his ever-shrinking alone time.

ENERGY

Although Amos says that he's kind of a dynamo and energy is rarely a problem, he frequently struggles with motivation and sometimes lacks a genuine desire to engage with his work. He believes that this is because he has so many conflicting priorities that by the time he manages to engage with one of them, he has to disengage and move on to something else. As such, it's difficult to ever feel like he's doing his best work. His life is full of work of various levels of urgency screaming for his attention.

STIMULI

Amos is required to regularly process truckloads of information. In addition to e-mail, phone calls, and face-to-face conversations, he's required to stay abreast of industry trends, process studies, and reports that may be helpful in making strategic decisions.

"Did you read this case study?"

"Have you connected with XYZ Learning Organization to get their thoughts?"

"A retired employee worked on an idea similar to this twenty-five years ago—you should give him a call to discuss it."

All of these are valuable leads that could help him generate ideas for his projects, but the sheer quantity of data to synthesize is overwhelming. He feels as though he's trying to drink from a fire hose.

HOURS

Much of Amos's time is spent in obligatory meetings discussing his projects, managing internal relationships, and dealing with other company priorities. "My plate is always American-sized, food falling off the sides," he explains. "Finding time to think during the day is nearly impossible. Thus, I have to work nights, let stuff go, or just accept that not everything I do can be great, even though that's the expectation." Amos feels like much of his time is spoken for, and there's precious little left to actually think about the work.

Amos's situation is typical. It's reflective of conversations I've had with creatives in various roles and nearly every industry. The single contribution they feel most accountable for—bringing brilliant new insights and ideas into their business—is the first thing that gets squeezed out by the everyday demands of their role.

CREATIVE RHYTHM

To unleash your creative potential now and thrive over the long term, you need to establish your own rhythm—one that is independent of the pressures and expectations you face each day. This Creative Rhythm will provide you with the stability and clarity to engage your problems head-on. This rhythm is set by how you structure the five elements you observed in Amos's story above.

Focus

If we could harness the sum total of wasted energy each day in the workplace, we could probably power the earth for a year. There is so much ineffective work because there is often a lack of clarity around what we're really trying to do. In order to create effectively, you need a clear and concrete understanding of your objectives. In chapter 4 you will learn how to weed out urgent but unimportant activities, and how to direct your efforts toward only those things that will increase your level of creative engagement.

Relationships

One of the most powerful sources of creative inspiration and rejuvenation is other people. Unfortunately, many successful creatives are haphazard about their relationships and only intentionally build on them when the stars align or when it's otherwise convenient or expedient. When you go "outside yourself," it frees you up and unlocks latent parts of your creativity. If you want to thrive, you need to systematically engage with other people, in part to be reminded that life is bigger than your immediate problems. In chapter 5 you will learn how to be purposeful about the relationships in your life, how to build creatively stimulating friendships, and how to limit access to the creativity vampires.

Energy

Simple time management is not enough. It does you no good to micromanage your time down to the last second if you don't have the energy to remain fully engaged for that time. To make the most of your day, you need to establish practices around energy management. In chapter 6 you will learn how to account for energy in your daily life and how to build bulwarks against some of the more pervasive energy drains.

Stimuli

The quality of the output of any process is dependent on the quality of its inputs, and this holds true for the creative process. I call creative inputs "stimuli" because they stimulate creative thought. Despite their importance, remarkably few people are intentional about the kinds of stimuli they absorb on a day-to-day basis. If you want to regularly generate brilliant ideas, you must be purposeful about what you are putting into your head. As the old saying goes, "Garbage in, garbage out." In chapter 7 you will learn how to ensure that you are getting good creative nutrition.

Hours

Time is the currency of productivity, and how you handle it will ultimately determine your success or failure. But in order to really thrive, you need to shake yourself of our collective obsession with time efficiency and learn instead to focus on effectiveness. You need to ensure that the practices that truly make you a more effective creator are making it onto your calendar. In chapter 8 you will learn how to ensure that your time is being spent effectively and to great result.

Practices in each of these five areas (F-R-E-S-H) provide the foundation for a life that is prolific, brilliant, and healthy. In later chapters, we will dive deeply into each of these. But there are obstacles we face on the road to everyday brilliance. Often these pitfalls are the result of organizational tensions that inevitably emerge whenever there is an attempt to organize the creative process or to instill systems around creative work.

POSSIBILITIES VERSUS PRAGMATICS

To create is to explore possibilities. There are a nearly infinite number of possible solutions to any given problem, and if you explore long enough you will almost always uncover another one. In many ways, the creative process is a never-ending chase after the possible. You have permission to think big about your projects, to dream and to innovate. You are told to really stretch yourself and to try to come up with something truly new. This creates a kind of "race to brilliance" with each new project.

But no matter what is said, the reality is that your work life is full of constraints. You have deadlines, budget limitations, and client requirements to deal with. The result is that you probably often feel pulled back and forth between possibilities and pragmatics. On the one hand, the lure of another conceptual breakthrough is seductive, but on the other, you must deal with the reality that your work is being both timed and judged.

> **"You can't wait for inspiration, you have to go after it with a club."**
>
> **—Jack London**

The pull between possibilities and pragmatics has us serving two masters at once. Even as we're exploring some new idea and getting really excited about our direction, we hear the little voice in the back of our head asking us, "Are you sure you want to try this? This is risky!" So we don't go quite as far as we might. Over time, as we deal with more and more of these practical compromises, we feel the effects on our creative drive. Our passion wanes, because it's difficult to stay excited about the work when we feel that practical limitations will ultimately prevent us from really doing something we believe to be truly great.

Both creatives and organizations are constantly dealing with this tension. Organizations recognize the need to give creatives permission to innovate and explore, but they also realize that boundaries are necessary to ensure the sustainability of the organization. No one is to blame here—it's just a reality—but it can feel very frustrating. Creatives are hired because of their capacity to create value for the organization, yet they frequently feel they must navigate a series of hurdles in order to do their best work.

How does this affect your creativity? You probably feel the pressure to be brilliant and—at the same time—to be practical. These are conflicting tensions, and they are the source of most of the burnout, frustration, and organizational strife I've seen within creative organizations. It's such a significant factor that we're going to tackle it in depth in the next chapter.

THE DYNAMICS OF TEAM WORK

**In 2005, military strategist Thomas Barnett took the** stage at the TED Conference, a gathering of intellectuals, innovators, and artists, to share some bold thoughts about the current state of the U.S. military. According to Barnett, there are two fundamental roles played by any military force: advancing in order to take new ground and occupying the ground after it has been taken. The challenge that military strategists perpetually wrestle with is how to train and equip a force to do both effectively. Each role demands a unique set of skills, and there is an intricate balance between the two. Without a "leviathan" force (as Barnett calls the force that takes new ground), there is no need for an occupying force, and to require soldiers who are trained to aggressively take ground to do the largely administrative work of occupying that ground is challenging to both the soldiers and the overall mission.

As creatives, we are wired to take new ground. We love the

thrill of the chase, pursuing objectives and tackling goals that seem just beyond our reach. We are fundamentally wired to be a part of the leviathan force, or we would never have chosen jobs that require so much self-definition. Much of our time as organizational creatives, however, is spent occupying the ground that we've already taken. We must deal with systems, processes, and protocol in executing our ideas. We have to deal with the everyday demands of communicating and creating interdependently. While we certainly gain new opportunities when we organize around the creative process, we must also deal with the inherent limitations and side effects of collaborative creative work.

THE PROS AND CONS OF TEAM CREATING

Organizations organize. It's their reason for being. And organization is good, because it allows groups of people to leverage assets more efficiently and scale in ways that aren't possible for individuals. Many people have brilliant ideas, but unless they are capable of organizing around those ideas, it will be impossible for them to get much of any significance done. As much as we may venerate the ideal of the lone innovator, slaving away in the garage or studio to bring a vision to life, the reality is that most of the time brilliant creations are the result of teams of people stumbling awkwardly into the unknown.

> As creatives, we are wired to take new ground. We love the thrill of the chase, pursuing objectives and tackling goals that seem just beyond our reach.

Scott Belsky is CEO of Behance, a New York–based company dedicated to helping creatives execute their ideas, and author of *Making Ideas Happen*. Belsky believes that "the greatest breakthroughs across all industries are a result of creative people and teams that are especially productive." A significant factor in their productivity, Belsky has discovered, is their ability to organize. In most work, a well-organized team of creatives—even if they are not highly skilled—will produce exponentially more and better results than a lone genius. Strong organization is critical for teams of people who want to accomplish great things in the world, and a critical element of that organization is the ability to lead by establishing a culture obsessed with execution. Belsky continues, "History is made by passionate, creative people and organizations with the rare ability to lead others—and themselves."

While important, effective organization alone is not sufficient to ensure the success of a creative team. An environment must be established that offers sufficient resources, fosters the right organizational mind-set, and allows for the natural ebb and flow of the creative process—because creative productivity is naturally rhythmic, and there will be periods of incredible productivity followed by periods when it seems like we can't think our way out of a paper bag. For those of us who work primarily on our own, this is not much of a challenge because we have the flexibility to adjust our work life as needed, but for those of us who work in a team context this can be a lot more challenging. We don't have the luxury of having an "off day," and when we do have one the entire team suffers. None of us are machines, and there will always be an element of unpredictability about our work.

There are a few creativity-draining tensions that result from any attempt to organize creative work. Some of these tensions have become so engrained in our workplace experience that they just seem like the natural order of things, but once we learn to spot them, we can establish practices to counteract them. In this chapter we're going to examine the dynamics of organizational creative work and how they affect our ability to be consistently brilliant and effective.

CONTRADICTORY EXPECTATIONS

Creative teams face two conflicting pressures: to produce timely and consistent work, and to produce unique and brilliant work. The pull between these two expectations creates a tension like that from two people pulling on a rope. When this pull—between possibilities and pragmatics—becomes too strong, the rope is taut, eliminating the peaks and troughs of productivity required do our best creative work.

We are constantly forced to choose between striving to improve the quality of our work and driving it to completion. This dynamic manifests itself in three tensions: the time-versus-value tension, the predictable-versus-rhythmic tension, and the product-versus-process tension.

The Time-Versus-Value Tension

The traditional model of compensation is based on time. A worker exchanges a certain number of hours per week for a fair wage. If you are a good worker, you work hard all day long for your paycheck, and then at quitting time you go home and forget about your job for the evening.

As a creative worker, you're not really paid for your time, you're paid for the value you create. Just showing up and doing a set of tasks every day doesn't cut it. You are required to perpetually create new value in order to prove your worth to your employer, your peers, and even to yourself. And though many creatives have more flexibility than ever regarding how and where they do their work, this flexibility introduces a new kind of performance pressure: completion anxiety. Because we're capable of working at all times—our mind goes with us everywhere, after all—we continue working on our projects for as long as we possibly can. We're never really certain when we've done enough.

> "An idea that is developed and put into action is more important than an idea that exists only as an idea."
> —Edward de Bono, creativity expert and author of *Lateral Thinking*

In order to pacify this insecurity, many of us find that we're working even when we're supposed to be off the clock. Just a little more research. Just one more brainstorming session. Just a few more minutes tweaking the proposal. It is a never-ending pursuit of value creation.

In spite of the increasing flexibility that many workplaces are introducing and the growing number of freelancers, many of us are actually working more hours than ever because it's so difficult to draw the line between work time and nonwork time. And because we are not just doing repeatable processes, each project we're working on requires something new from us. The pressure to keep the momentum going on our projects can feel a bit like pushing a rock up a very steep hill. We might stop to sit and to catch our breath, but we still have to exert a small amount of effort at all times to keep the rock from rolling back down the hill.

There are a few questions that this time-versus-value tension forces us to wrestle with.

Am I proving my worth?

This question keeps performance-driven people up at night. We wonder if we could have done more, or if we will be recognized for what we did. We wonder if our career is on track, and we think that perhaps if we just do that one more thing it will push us over the top for our next promotion. And now that we have technology to keep us connected to our work and our peers at all times, there is always one more thing that we can do right now to move the ball forward. We have eliminated the off switch. We're on all the time.

One creative director often found himself up at very early hours checking e-mail, sometimes even turning on his phone, which he kept next to his bed, in the middle of the night just to check if anything noteworthy was going on. Additionally, responding to e-mail was typically the last thing he did before going to bed each night, making it difficult to slow his mind and rest.

This perpetual inbox obsession wasn't an organizational expectation; rather, it was fueled by a deep insecurity that something important was going to happen and that he wouldn't respond in time to contribute meaningfully to the conversation. He admitted that it was rare that this behavior had actually increased his performance, but that it was really just a kind of pacifier to help him feel wired-in and needed. He was always concerned about whether he was adding enough value to the company. He implemented some of the techniques in the forthcoming chapters on focus and energy, including setting dedicated (but frequent) times for checking e-mail and buffers before bedtime to allow his mind to slow before sleep. Gradually he felt his energy level and creative performance rise as a result.

While there are certainly career-related factors that drive this insecurity, the drive to produce goes beyond the desire to be a good employee. We want to know that what we're doing matters. We want to know that if we were to disappear tomorrow, someone would notice. In a sense, we feel like we define our space in the world as we create value. Unhealthy? Probably. But often true nonetheless.

What kind of value should I create?

As a creative, you probably have latitude in defining your course of action on your projects. You may have a general sense of direction or some objectives, but you continually face the question: *What do I do next?*

This introduces the pressure to get it right each time, because there is tremendous opportunity cost associated with getting it wrong. It's possible to spend hours or even days heading down the wrong trail if you make one bad choice about where you should be spending your time and energy. This pressure can be paralyzing, especially when you're working on critical and timely work.

I was once involved in an off-site team-building session designed to teach better methods for collaboration. For one exercise we went out into the woods for a little "orienteering." We were broken into teams and tasked with finding an object hidden in the woods using only a compass and a set of instructions unique to our starting position. Pride was on the line as my teammates and I hurriedly worked our way through the first few instructions.

"Forty-five degrees northwest, twenty paces."

"Due south, thirty-five paces."

We practically ran through the first several steps before realizing that we were a significant distance from everyone else. Our initial thought was that perhaps we were the only geniuses in the bunch, but we quickly concluded that we were actually the ones who'd messed up—in a big way.

As we backed our way through the previous instructions, we realized that we'd been off by a few degrees in one of the first few steps. Now that we were several instructions down the list, the compounding effect of that one mistake had led us significantly off course.

In a similar way, one wrong decision early in a project can significantly affect the end value of your work. As a result, the pressure to determine the right *kind* of value to produce can become paralyzing to your creative process.

Who is responsible for what?

Collaboration gives you the opportunity to accomplish more than you could alone, but it also introduces new complexity into the work. You must deal with the distribution of responsibilities across the team and with minor (or major) disagreements about the kind of value that's being created.

> **"Few things in life are less efficient than a group of people trying to write a sentence. The advantage of this method is that you end up with something for which you will not be personally blamed."**
> **—Scott Adams, creator of *Dilbert***

There's a lot of overlap in highly conceptual, creative work, which can result in redundancy, confusion, and disagreement. Also, because the tasks for the team must continually be defined, a high level of communication must be employed just to stay on course.

If it's difficult for you to answer questions about the value you're creating as an individual, it becomes vastly more difficult for teams to do so. Each member is wrestling with the same questions of how much value he should create and which tasks he should choose. Everyone is also rightly concerned with his own value to the company and whether he's doing enough to justify his continued employment. In unhealthy teams, this can result in a lot of posturing or blame shifting throughout a project, depending on whether it's going well or poorly. No one wants to be left without a chair when the music stops!

▶ THE EFFECTS OF THE TIME-VERSUS-VALUE TENSION

It can be very difficult to fully engage in your work when you aren't certain how to know when you're finished. When the main indicator of your performance is the amount of value you create, it's easy to feel like the work is never done. The behavior for many creative teams is to work until they simply run out of time.

One team I encountered had become addicted to last-minute

change. They would continue to tweak and change a project right up until it was delivered, often discarding weeks or even months of thought and preparation. While this sometimes had the short-term effect of an improved end product, the net long-term effect on the team was that people stopped thinking strategically at the beginning of the process, knowing that everything would likely change in the end anyway. Until it was pointed out, they didn't realize that this behavior was significantly affecting the overall value they created as a team. They were allowing a few minor improvements at the last minute to affect their larger sense of engagement as a team, and their work was suffering.

The tension to continually improve weighs on individual creatives as well. Because most of us are managing multiple projects simultaneously, there is always something we could be doing right now to move our work forward. It takes an incredible amount of willpower not to work when we are technically off the clock. Additionally, many of us love the work we do and would probably rather be working than doing any of the many other things we could be doing. We're actually *choosing* to work perpetually! We've adopted a working lifestyle. It's as natural to us as blinking and breathing.

In his masterwork *Creativity*, in which he profiles the life and work of brilliant creatives across a broad spectrum of fields, researcher and author Mihaly Csikszentmihalyi writes, "One thing about creative work is that it's never done. In different words, every person we interviewed said that it was equally true that they had worked every minute of their careers, and that they had never worked a day in all their lives. They experienced even the most focused immersion in extremely difficult tasks as a lark, an exhilarating and playful adventure."

It's true that there is often such an affinity for our work that we would choose it over other activities, even recreational ones. But in our pursuit of value creation it's possible to overwork our minds without obvious signs of distress. We don't have the same aches and pains that may accompany a day spent running a marathon or chopping wood. As a result, being aware of how mental overexertion is affecting us is often difficult, until we suddenly realize that we're not creating at the level we once did or that we're just not as excited about our work as we used to be.

You'll learn some ways to mitigate this time-versus-value tension in the chapters on focus, energy, and hours.

The Predictable-Versus-Rhythmic Tension

In a smaller organization, each worker wears multiple hats, and the order of the day is all about getting things done, regardless of how. But as the organization grows, some degree of predictability becomes necessary—to allocate resources, hire appropriately, and make reasonable promises to clients or customers. Consistent and predictable production makes it possible to analyze how efficiently individuals and systems are performing across the organization—as the company gets bigger, there is more to protect, and the pressure to not screw it up only grows over time.

But this need for predictability can begin to take a toll on those responsible for doing the work. While it's possible, even necessary, to measure the relationship of resources to output in highly systemized, repeatable work, like sales or manufacturing, it's nearly impossible to do so reliably for creative work. After all, how can we predict when business-changing insights will occur? How do you create a system that ensures that only the best ideas are executed, and that the not-so-good ones fade away? Because these problems depend on the discretion and insights of individuals, tension is inevitable.

This push toward systemized and predictable creativity can sometimes cause creatives to feel like we're expected to perform like machines. As a result, though we resent it, we often begin to behave that way. (No worries—we'll learn how to mitigate this in later chapters.)

> **Every organization begins as an advance force and ends up as an occupying force.**

Despite the negative effects on creative output, the organizational tendency is to gravitate toward predictable but still profitable productivity. One CEO told me that he calls this "bunting for singles": It's better to get on base consistently than to swing for the fence. Sure, swinging for the fence may yield a few home runs, but it's also going to result in a lot of strikeouts. In many organizations, victory is won and measured over decades, even if this is never outwardly expressed. Ultimately, the organization's instinct is to protect the ground that's already been taken rather than take new ground. Every organization begins as an advance force and ends up as an occupying force.

This is fine, as long as the expectations are consistent. But then we hear a mandate to be "innovative" and "shake things up." We feel the pressure to do something brilliant. To change the game. These mandates require unpredictability, risk, and unbalanced effort. They are directly contradictory to the systems the organization has set up, and we ultimately begin to feel the tension.

A highly productive creative process isn't at all predictable and is directly opposed to the "bunting for singles" ethic. In effective creating there are peaks and troughs. There are seasons of incredible productivity and there are seasons in between. But over the long term, a healthy, rhythmic creative process is capable of creating an *exponential* return on resources. The problem is that we often don't experience these exponential returns because we—or the organization—are not comfortable with the sometimes less productive times in the short term. In other words, in the effort to cut off the troughs we inadvertently cut off the peaks as well.

The rhythmic nature of a healthy creative process can be very uncomfortable for managers because of the constant pressure from the organization to be efficient. Efficiency doesn't allow for peaks and troughs, so managers sometimes try to ensure that there is at least the appearance of productivity at all times.

▶ SNAPSHOT PRODUCTIVITY

Imagine that, at some point in the next week, I show up randomly at your workplace and take a photo of you working. You don't know when I will appear, but I am going to base your salary and next promotion on the content of that snapshot. If I catch you at a time when you are especially productive, things will work out well for you. If I happen to catch you on a coffee break, you might want to start packing your things.

Does this sound a little silly and arbitrary? Of course. But a very similar thing happens within organizations. Because of the drive toward predictability and efficiency, there is a constant and worried eye toward the productivity of employees. But the way many organizations measure the productivity of creative workers often has more in common with how they would measure the productivity of a copier than of a person.

As I was standing in the back of the room after speaking at a conference, a design manager for a software company spotted me, got up from his seat, and made a beeline in my direction. From the look on his face, my first reaction was that he was angry about something I'd said. As he got closer I could see that he wasn't angry, just emotional. He expressed that this "machine-like" expectation was the norm within his organization but that he hadn't previously been able to put words to it. He had felt many times that the *appearance* of busyness was much more important than the actual work that was getting done. Preservation and predictability had become the norm, and expectations were set upon very recent performance versus contribution over time. He was excited to apply the practices I'd just taught in my keynote as a way to mitigate these pressures.

His experience is not unique. Many managers subconsciously take a snapshot of how someone is doing *right now* and use that as the metric for the worker's overall performance. What is potentially devastating is when the organization catches the creative at a peak of productivity. From that point forward there is an unspoken expectation that he will predictably produce at this high level of output. Everything he does in the future will be compared to this high point, and if he doesn't hit this mark he is deemed to be in a slump. For organizations, managers, or individual creatives to expect these kinds of peaks continually is to violate the very dynamics that allowed for this kind of high-level productivity to begin with!

▶ THE EFFECTS OF THE PREDICTABLE-VERSUS-RHYTHMIC TENSION

Because of the predictable-versus-rhythmic tension, expectations continue to rise. In the effort to make productivity predictable to the organization, our current work is benchmarked against our previous work. Over time, as a matter of self-protection, creatives begin to conserve their energy and take their shots where they seem most effective rather than pour themselves fully into their work, because they don't want to have to sustain such a high level of output over time. As a result, they plug along, meeting their objectives, but knowing deep down that they could do better work. This can cause them to feel disconnected from the work, from their coworkers, and from the organizational mission. They may even begin to feel contempt for the organization and feel used or entitled. (A word of caution: this is not the organization's fault. Organizations are made of people, and the people involved are typically doing what they think is the right thing for the overall organization. It's not personal, though it can feel intensely so.) The solution to all this is to regain a sense of mastery over time and focus, as we'll discuss in later chapters.

For leaders, expectation escalation can happen without our even realizing it. A key solution is to have regular conversations about expectations in order to ensure that everyone really understands what's expected. A few questions to include in these conversations are the following:

- Do you know what's expected of you right now? Tell me what you think are your top three priorities.
- What expectations do you have of me, and am I meeting them?

It takes guts to ask for the truth, but simply having these short, scheduled conversations can help teams avoid many of the pitfalls of the predictable-versus-rhythmic tension and can allow all members of the team to feel free to engage fully and creatively in their work.

The Product-Versus-Process Tension

The organization is primarily concerned with the finished product, but 99 percent of what we do as creatives is process. In fact, many creative jobs are fundamentally oriented around perpetuating processes rather than generating products. There are rarely times when we can hold something in our hands at the end of the day and say, "If I hadn't been here, this wouldn't exist." Instead, we are often one of many value-add laborers who contribute layers of creative work to a given project. Responsibility and accountability for our projects, especially in larger organizations, are often spread quite thin.

What's more, the final result of our creative work is typically judged subjectively, and by someone other than us. As a result, being able to gauge in the middle of the process whether what we're working on will please our "judge" can often be difficult. We frequently engage in the entire creative process and emerge on the other side with a finished product only to hear our client or manager say, "Yeah . . . I kind of get what you're going for here, but it's just not quite there yet." It can be difficult to understand what to do with this kind of input, and chances are that the manager is probably struggling just as much as we are for a direction on what to do next.

Yes, this is to be expected. We're being paid to do a job. But over time this dynamic can tempt us to gravitate toward doing whatever will get approved rather than taking risks and exploring as we're creating. We do less than we're capable of because we don't want to deal with the consequences of disapproval at the end of the process.

One editor described this as "never knowing what's over the next hill." She said that she's more than willing to work hard, but that it's difficult to fully expend herself creatively when she's not certain that her work will result in approval, especially when objectives are less than clear. As a result, she tended to ignore her own creative discretion and would instead just do whatever she thought was likely to "make the cut." I was able to help her build specific conversations about objectives with her manager into her weekly rituals to ensure that the manager was staying in touch with her process, rather than just checking in at the beginning and the end of a project. These simple checkpoints helped her engage more fully and in confidence, knowing that project milestones and objectives were clear.

In many ways, this process of developing ideas is similar to the childbirth process. First there is a brief and ecstatic moment of "conception." We have a flash of insight when two or more idea fragments combine to form a new and better one: the "creative accident." Although this is typically the most attractive part of the process, it is only the very beginning. The idea hasn't really taken form yet; it's still just an impression in our mind. Many ideas never get past the moment of conception because they aren't acted upon.

Assuming that we decide to move forward with our idea, there will next be a period of gestation in which the idea takes form. This is the real work of creating. We gradually develop the idea, building on the initial inspiration, refining it through multiple iterations. We will often collaborate with others. This can be a very challenging time. There will be highs and lows. We may go through periods of alternating excitement and loathing for our work. Success depends on our persistence and our willingness to keep refining and iterating even when we feel like moving on to something new. Many teams fail because they are unable to persist.

Commitment to the process is critical in this gestation period. While many organizations treat it like a linear progression toward the end product, great creative work requires risk and experimentation, which means some degree of unpredictability. For example, when an advertising agency lands a new client, the project is thrown into a pipeline with defined steps and a specific time frame for accomplishing certain tasks. It's a very linear process: establish objectives, set the scope, generate ideas, develop concepts, pitch concepts to the client, go through approvals, production, et cetera. Because of the organization's need for a degree of predictability, these pipelines must be in place. But the tension is that each of these stages of the pipeline is filled with experimentation, risk, and trial and error. While to the organization "develop concept for ABC campaign" is a two-day process, the artificial establishment of a time line doesn't account for the unpredictability of what happens during this time. In other words, it doesn't account for the true dynamics of *process*, and thus the creatives feel the tension to be brilliant, but to be so within the arbitrarily imposed deadline.

> The "conception" and "birth" of our ideas are small book-
> ends to the real work of creating—the process.

Eventually, if we stick with it, we will have a finished product. The "birth" of our idea as a finished product is the end result of a very long process and, as with a newborn, rarely looks like what we imagined it would. The process often takes us to new and unexpected places in our work. The "conception" and "birth" of our ideas are small bookends to the real work of creating—the process.

Why is this important? Because many organizations spend a lot of energy both on generating ideas and vetting the finished product, but very little time and effort creating healthy systems and expectations around the bulk of the work, which is the long process between idea and product. This is why Accidental Creative spends so much time working with creative teams to help them establish an "idea culture," meaning a culture that values the process of perpetual idea generation and development, rather than one that's driven solely by the end product.

▶ THE EFFECTS OF THE PRODUCT-VERSUS-PROCESS TENSION

It can be very challenging to spend days or weeks in a process only to have your finished work judged in a thirty-minute client review or a sit-down meeting with your manager's manager. There are many decisions you had to make in order to arrive at the finished product, but most of those decisions are invisible to your judge. The only results they experience are the finished product and whatever words you can use to justify why it ended up the way it is. This is, of course, what you're being paid for, but the experience of having weeks of work judged in a matter of minutes is de-motivating to say the least.

One friend relayed to me that the internal creatives in his company call the decision makers "vampires," because they tend to suck all the creative energy out of the room. In a project-review session there is a defined review process—from juniormost to seniormost, in rank order—when offering opinions on the finished product. By the end of these sessions, creatives are often left with a lot of feedback on their finished product but little understanding of the mind-set that led to the feedback. In other words, the conversation focuses more on product than on process, which contributes significantly to the tension between the two in this particular organization.

The tension between product and process is a natural tension within any kind of organized creative work, so we can't ignore its effects. We can, however, learn to mitigate them by applying principles related to time, focus, and relationships, which we'll discuss in later chapters.

There are a few side effects that result from working in the three tensions discussed in this chapter. In order to do your most effective work, you must understand how these side effects derail your creative process and how to spot them before they take root. That's the subject of the next chapter.

THE SIDE EFFECTS: DEALING WITH THE ASSASSINS OF CREATIVITY

 **3.** **Imagine that one day you hear a knocking in your** car's engine. Even though it's annoying, there seems to be nothing mechanically wrong with your car—it still drives, stops, and turns just fine—so you choose to ignore it. But one day, while on a busy highway, your car suddenly breaks down in the fast lane, and there's no median to navigate to for safety. You're unexpectedly in a very precarious situation. Though it seems to have happened all of a sudden, it all began when you chose to ignore the obvious warning signs several weeks before.

Similarly, whenever we choose to ignore the warning signs that we are violating the natural rhythms of the creative process, either by choice or because of our work environment, there will be unhealthy side effects. We can often go for weeks at a time without feeling them, but we will eventually begin to experience these drawbacks: apathy, discontent, boredom, exhaustion, frustration, a general lack of ideas. Working in the create-on-demand world, expected to be constantly on, you probably experience each of these side effects on a regular basis. Just like your car may continue to run for a while in disrepair, you can be very effective in short bursts, even violating your natural rhythms for a time, but eventually the negative side effects will catch up to you in the form of these symptoms.

While creative workplaces are very complex and there are many dynamics at play, there are three damaging side effects that serve as broad categories for all the others. I like to call them the "assassins" of the creative process, because they are stealthy and they effectively neutralize our creative capacity. They can creep into a work environment almost unseen and begin to undo our capacity to perform at our best. Once you understand these assassins and can spot their effects, you can begin to systematically weed them out.

The three assassins of the creative process are dissonance, fear, and expectation escalation. While each of these dynamics is present in varying degrees in every organization, for some teams and creatives they have become a way of life. The net result is a workplace in which rationalization and mediocrity become the norm. Innovation is often the rallying cry, but bunting for singles is the everyday ethic.

So let's meet the enemies.

DISSONANCE: IT JUST DOESN'T ADD UP

While watching a movie, have you ever had a sense that something bad is about to happen to the character on screen? Often this sense of impending doom has little to do with the visual cues of the film and more to do with the soundtrack. The subtle music playing throughout the scene sends cues that something isn't right. One of the tools that film composers use to create this effect is *dissonance*. Dissonance is a musical term used to describe two notes played simultaneously that seem as if they don't belong together and don't resolve. This creates a kind of musical tension, and because the human mind craves resolution of unresolved patterns, it waits expectantly for that resolution, which never comes. If used effectively, dissonance can make an absolutely benign scene of a woman walking down a hallway into an edge-of-your-seat thrill ride.

> **"Sometimes the questions are complicated and the answers are simple."**
>
> **—Dr. Seuss**

Resolving dissonance is one of the main functions of creative thought. We are quick to notice when things don't add up. But while it's usually helpful when used to solve the creative problems in your life and work, this ability to recognize and resolve patterns can also provide unwanted distractions to your creative process. You have only so much capacity to process data, and when there is a high amount of dissonance in your environment, it can rob you of some of that capacity. You can spend a lot of time spinning your wheels trying to resolve things that are ultimately unresolvable.

Organizational dissonance is rampant within many creative workplaces. The most significant dissonance within organizations exists when the "why" of our work isn't lining up with the "what" of our day-to-day activity. When this happens our minds go to work to try to resolve these misalignments, and much of our creative problem-solving bandwidth is hijacked by our mind's need to resolve these environmental incongruities. These points of dissonance cause us to feel perpetually uneasy and make it difficult for us to know how to engage in our work. For example:

"We deliver innovative solutions to clients!" (But just give the clients whatever they ask for.)

"We value team and collaboration!" (But really, just do what we tell you and don't ask questions.)

"We value our people!" (But we're going to have to ask you to work again this weekend.)

In his book *How the Mighty Fall*, author and researcher Jim Collins claims that one of the first signs of the decline of many great companies is when they fail to recognize the "why" behind their day-to-day activities. Once an organization has lost sight of this important connection, it inevitably gravitates toward mediocrity. He says, "When institutions fail to distinguish between current practices and the enduring principles of their success, and mistakenly fossilize around their practices, they've set themselves up for decline."

One of the most important responsibilities of a creative leader is to eliminate these little areas of dissonance as often as possible. They need to ensure that the "why" and the "what" are lining up for people on their team by consistently reminding team members of the overall strategy and how it aligns with their current day-to-day work. Doing this helps creative workers stay focused and energized, and eases the subterranean dissonance that can quickly emerge when doing complex work.

So where do you find this dissonance? There are three major sources. By monitoring each of these we can effectively reduce the degree to which dissonance zaps creative effectiveness.

Unnecessary Complexity

Hello, my name is Todd, and I am a recovering complexity junkie. I tend to complicate things when I feel uncomfortable or insecure. It's a defensive measure; I'll do anything to avoid being seen as uncertain. A few years ago, a coworker called me out on my complexity addiction, and ever since then I have kept a printout of the following on my office door:

$$1 + 1 = [\, [\, (9 \times 3) \, / \, 3 \,] \, / \, 3 \,] - 1$$

You'll notice that the formula balances, but that the right side of the equation adds a lot of steps and unnecessary complexity. It's there to remind me that the simplest approach is always the best place to start, and it's the first thing I see when I arrive at work each day.

Unnecessary complexity is an unfortunate, but natural, result of organizational growth. Things are very simple in the early stages of a business. There are few people involved, and everyone has to be a generalist. It's very entrepreneurial, and everyone is very close to the "main thing" for the company. It's easy to see how individual efforts contribute to the overall objectives of the company. It may be challenging to keep up, but the rules are pretty simple: Do your job, whatever it takes.

As the company grows, however, there is more and more demand for specialization. Divisions are created and silos are established to manage different areas of business. Each division has its main thing, which is a subset of the overall main thing. People are hired within these divisions, and they also have their individual objectives and responsibilities. Systems are established, goals and quotas are implemented, and workers dive deeply into their highly specialized work. Some of these workers are now three, or four, or five steps away from the central objectives of the company. There are objectives upon objectives, and systems upon systems. It can get very complex. It becomes easy to grow confused about how we should prioritize our work and even what we're really trying to do when we have to navigate a matrix of priorities just to develop a simple task list.

"Making the simple complicated is commonplace;
making the complicated simple, awesomely simple,
that's creativity."

—Charles Mingus

But this kind of unnecessary complexity isn't limited to companies and teams. Inventing chaos is a common defense mechanism early in the creative process, especially when we're uncertain about what we're trying to do. Even worse, sometimes we introduce complexity into the later stages of the project by adopting new ideas or strategies that create undue stress. We make things very complex in order to mask the reality that, deep down, we're confused about our true objectives. Some of us (myself included) use unnecessary complexity as a mask for insecurity. (If we aren't certain we can nail the project, we'll at least confuse the heck out of them and show them how smart we are.) This is a waste of creative brainpower and does nothing to get us closer to our objectives.

Several years ago I was leading an organizational restructure that involved bringing other departments onto my team. Because of the new people on the team, it was a perfect time to revisit our workflow and to develop new systems for getting our work done, but I was uncertain about exactly what that should look like. It was my first time leading this kind of effort, and I was nervous about what failure might mean for everyone involved. As a result, I subconsciously created problems where none existed—and solved them—so that I could feel like I was making progress. All I was doing was creating busywork where none existed in order to avoid making the hard decisions necessary to finish the reorganization. This made the entire process much more difficult for everyone involved, and especially for me.

But unnecessary complexity is not always the result of insecurity or uncertainty. Sometimes it's simply a function of growth. As organizations grow, new systems are needed to move the work forward. Over time, these systems can become antiquated, but because they've been around for so long, no one thinks to ask the question. Is this really the best way? Systems pile upon systems, and soon people within the organization develop compensatory behaviors in order to get around these unnecessarily complex systems. This means a lot of wasted creative energy goes toward figuring out the system rather than toward the actual work of the organization.

You need to be diligent about asking yourself, "Can I make this process more simple?" Because there will always be a lot of complexity that is beyond your control, you must ensure that those places where you have influence are streamlined and aligned. You must also get comfortable with eliminating things in your life that are getting in the way of clarity and focus. (I will give you some strategies for how to do this in the chapter on focus.)

Question: **Are there unnecessarily complex systems in your life and work right now? Are there ways you can simplify them?**

Unclear Objectives

There is an area outside one of our favorite restaurants where our children love to run around and play. After dinner we will often give them time to burn off their excess energy before bed by playing games. Our two young boys love to race each other, and our daughter always wants to get in on the action. Unfortunately for the boys, she is not content to simply be a participant; she needs to referee, too. She will run around in circles, with the boys following her lead, until she stops, throws her hands in the air, and shouts, "I win!" Our older son is a strict rule follower and—of course—finds this totally unacceptable. After all, how can she declare herself the winner when there were no established rules? After many arguments and near brawls, we had to explain to the kids that it might be a good idea to clarify the rules of the game before they start playing. If they don't, how will they know what "winning" even looks like?

> **You must get comfortable with eliminating things in your life that are getting in the way of clarity and focus.**

In principle this sounds obvious, but this same dynamic plays out every day in the workplace, and it's a common source of organizational dissonance. Even though we've talked about a project extensively, the objectives are still unclear, and we're uncertain about what we're *really* trying to do. It's astounding to me how often I encounter people who are stuck on a creative problem and can't articulate what they're trying to accomplish. They have no idea what a "win" will look like. They're just running around in circles and waiting for someone to declare that the game is over.

This problem stems from our difficulty parsing *project* strategy from *creative* strategy. Project strategy boils down to the five *W*'s: *Why? Who? What? When? Where?* The creative strategy lies in *how* we plan to accomplish these objectives. Often, when we're trying to solve a creative problem, we jump straight to *how* we're going to do it, the creative strategy, before we've even settled on a concrete set of objectives, a project strategy.

When we do this, we are significantly handicapping our ability to effectively solve the problem. If we want to set ourselves up for success and eliminate dissonance, we must learn to set project objectives by answering the five *W*'s. The more comprehensively we define our objectives, the more likely we are to experience creative insight. We are giving our minds a set of constraints to work within.

For every project, answer the following questions to determine the project strategy:

Why? Why are we undertaking this work? What purpose does it serve?

Who? Whose approval is required? Who needs to be involved in the work? Who are we reaching?

What? What are we really trying to accomplish with this project? (No consultant-speak. Be very concrete.)

When? What are the hard (and soft) deadlines for the work? When will it be implemented?

Where? Where will the work be done? Where will the results of work appear?

Finally, once—and *only* once—we've established the project strategy we can work on the creative strategy:

How? How will we accomplish these objectives? What is the most appropriate way to solve these problems?

Because so many teams begin with execution (creative strategy) and skip over the objectives (project strategy), dissonance creeps into the work. We must make certain that the *why* (project strategy) and the *how* (creative strategy) line up.

A web-design firm I encountered said that one complexity of their work is that many clients come to them with specific executions—"Build us a website that . . ." or "We want an app that does . . ."—rather than objectives. As a result, they frequently have to adjust the clients' ingoing expectations enough to have a clear conversation about what their objectives truly are. This often changes the entire direction of their work, because once the objectives are clear, it becomes obvious that there are solutions available that the clients would never have thought of on their own. Overall, though they're initially suspicious about this objectives-clarifying process, clients are typically thrilled with the results.

Challenge: **Think of a problem you're currently working on, or one on which you are currently stuck creatively. Can you effectively and concretely answer the five *W*'s: *Why? Who? What? When? Where?* Or are you starting with execution: *How?***

Opacity

A third source of dissonance in creative teams is opacity, the result of key strategy and creative decisions being made in a "secret chamber," and then handed down to the rest of the organization for execution with little or no explanation of *why*. The more opaque the decision-making process, the more likely that misinterpretation and misalignment will follow.

In the physical world, a vacuum wants to be filled. In the same way, when there is a lack of explanation of *why* things are a certain way, we will often fill in that vacuum with whatever makes the most sense to us. That doesn't mean, however, that our understanding of why we are doing something lines up with our manager's why. As a result, we can spin our wheels trying to solve a problem without a true understanding of what we're really being asked to do. These little incongruities affect our creating, clouding our thinking.

> **The more opaque the decision-making process, the more likely that misinterpretation and misalignment will follow.**

One design firm had concentrated much of its client interactions in the hands of very few people. This isn't atypical, but in this case the firm's creative leaders were not very good about communicating client expectations, or key decisions about the direction of the project, to those actually doing the design work. Rather than explaining the reasoning behind the decisions, there would often be vague and unsupported requests to "clean this up" or "make that element slightly more dominant." This created a lot of dissonance for the junior designers as they attempted to do the work without understanding why they were being asked for specific changes. I helped these leaders understand that being more specific about the reason for their direction—for example, "The client thinks the design is too busy" or "The client wants this to draw more attention to itself"—would help clarify the objectives and allow their designers to introduce other potential solutions.

While there are certainly reasons to keep sensitive information under wraps, the clearer the organization can be about why decisions are made, the better.

Challenge: **Take a minute to look at your organization's current priorities. Can you explain why these priorities are currently the most important, or is there a lack of alignment between the** *why* **and the** *how* **of the work you're doing?**

Although the examples we described above are largely organizational, the principle of dissonance as a creativity assassin plays out in every area of our life. If you can better align the *why* and the *how* in your life, you will experience more creative accidents.

For example, there may be many activities that you continue to engage in long after they have ceased to be effective to your current work. They are artifacts from old goals, projects, or relationships, but they have nothing to do with what's currently important to you. You are simply doing them as a matter of habit. The result is that your daily activity isn't aligned with what is really important to you right now, and it creates complexity that you must navigate in order to do your work. We will be addressing how to eliminate these misalignments and ensure that your efforts match your objectives in the next chapter.

Question: **Are there systems you're still using that are ineffective for your current work but that you're using as a matter of habit rather than by purposeful choice?**

FEAR: THE INVISIBLE CEILING

Humans have evolved with a set of traits that made it possible for our ancestors to form social groups, develop new technologies, and outwit their enemies. Unfortunately, these are the same attributes that can inhibit our creativity. The most damaging of these hardwired traits is fear.

In some circumstances, fear is undeniably a useful tool. For example, if I'm standing on the edge of a hundred-foot cliff, I should feel a little fear and take a step or two back. I also want my kids to have a healthy respect for traffic so that they avoid the street when playing. These types of fear are and always have been crucial to our survival.

But there are other types of fear that, when allowed to dictate our behavior, can cause us to perform at significantly lower levels than our true capabilities. We project negative consequences to our behavior and limit our engagement out of a fear of what might happen, no matter how unlikely.

In his book *The Now Habit*, about fighting procrastination, Dr. Neil Fiore describes an experiment he performs with his patients to help them identify when they are behaving irrationally because of fear. He asks them to imagine that there is a wood plank lying across the floor, twenty feet long and six inches wide. He asks them if they would be able to walk across this plank without falling off. Inevitably, the patients respond that walking across this plank would be no problem. Fiore then asks them to imagine that the plank has been elevated to a height of one hundred feet in the air and is suspended between two buildings. He again asks the patients if they believe they could walk across the plank without falling off. This time, however, very few of the patients are willing to "walk the plank."

What has changed? Certainly not the technical skill required for the task. It's the same plank. But for some reason the respondents are now hesitant to walk across it. The only thing that has changed is the consequence of making a mistake. Suddenly, a slight misstep will mean death . . . or at least several broken bones. The perceived consequence of a mistake caused the respondents to choose not to engage in an activity that, only moments before, they had deemed easy.

Sound familiar? It's often the case that because of a fear of what *might* happen if they make a mistake, creatives play it safe. They elevate the potential consequences of making a mistake to unhealthy (and unrealistic) levels and, in order to avoid those consequences, do mediocre work.

For some of us, this fear is a natural result of our environment. I have worked with a few creatives who have been told point-blank, "If you screw this up, you're fired." But in my experience, that is a rare exception. For the most part, our fears are largely exaggerated; few of us can point to a person who lost his job because of a reasonable idea that didn't pan out. More often than not, we simply don't want to stand out, whether positively or negatively, because of the fear of being ostracized by our peers or managers.

This kind of fear can be corralled into two categories: fear of failure and, even worse, fear of success.

Fear of Failure

When we think of fear, this is probably the kind that comes to mind. We become risk averse because we don't want to come up short. We've been doing what we do for long enough that we understand how to do passable work in a risk-free way, so why take the chance on doing something more? But brilliant creative work is always the result of risk. In order to succeed, we must reach beyond our present circumstances and take chances that our work might fail. Peter Block, author of *The Answer to How Is Yes* and *Community*, told me in an interview that we must grow comfortable "living in the margins rather than in the center."

What are we *really* risking when we create? We might fear losing our job, but more often we're concerned about being perceived as inadequate or ineffective. We're afraid that no one will want to work with us on future projects. We're worried about our reputation.

This fear is not completely unfounded. If we push ourselves to go beyond the tried and true, others will inevitably think some of our ideas are bad. But in the end, the consequences of never taking creative risks will be significantly greater than some of our peers thinking we have poor taste. A lifetime of mediocrity is a high price to pay for safety. Paranoia undoes greatness.

> **A lifetime of mediocrity is a high price to pay for safety.**
> **Paranoia undoes greatness.**

You need to push through those places where it's easier to gravitate toward comfort instead of aggressively pursuing your best work. riCardo Crespo, Senior Vice President and Global Creative Chief for Twentieth Century Fox FCP, told me that his best advice for creatives is to "know your comfort zone and to work hard to stay out of it." Sharing from his personal experience, he said that a desire for comfort is the "single biggest factor that causes many creatives to shrink back from opportunity" and the biggest block to creative growth.

When we curtail our creative engagement out of a fear of what others will think, we are "elevating the plank." We are exaggerating the potential consequences of a mistake. So rather than doing something that we're wired for, something we're passionate about, or something that we believe could really make a difference, we back away from the ledge. We settle. We accept mediocrity.

It's conceivable that none of this is new information. We know that it's unlikely that we're going to be fired for a bad idea, but we're still reserved and often hold back from bringing ourselves fully to the creative process. Fear can have a strong hold over our engagement. In *Linchpin*, author Seth Godin argues that this is the result of something called the "lizard brain," the primal part of our brain that causes us to shrink back from anything that is perceived as a threat. We are hardwired to stay close to the herd and blend in as much as possible. After all, in the animal world the members of a tribe that stand out are often eaten first.

But we must learn to identify and circumvent the impulse of our survival instinct. To do so requires both awareness and the discipline to take calculated creative risks. We must practice taking risks when the stakes are lower so that we can perform when the pressure is on and it really matters. We'll talk about this more as we discuss best practices.

Question: **Where is fear of failure causing you to curtail your creative engagement? Where are you refusing to take risks in your work? What are the perceived consequences that are holding you back, and do you think they're real or imagined?**

Fear of Success

There is a second and more subversive form of fear that I've seen at work in many creatives. In your head, it sounds something like this:

Do I really want to knock this one out of the park? Do I really want to set myself up for that kind of future expectation? What will everyone else think? Will I be able to continue to sustain that pace? Can I continue to provide creative insight at that level? Maybe I should pace myself instead.

None of these thoughts are necessarily conscious, but they flit through our minds as we go about our work. This kind of fear plays on the paranoia that we can't continue to perform at a certain level of expectation or deal with the ongoing execution of an idea once it's launched. As a result we are hesitant to engage fully because we don't want to get in over our heads or deal with the consequences of success.

Fear of success can become an epidemic within creative teams. A blind eye is turned toward subpar performance, and there's a strong "you scratch my back, I'll scratch yours" ethic in which everyone rationalizes team members' work as great in order to maintain stability and avoid stretching themselves. The rationale is that by doing this we can lower expectations across the board, resulting in less risk of sustained future expectations for us and for our team. It sounds ridiculous on the surface, but I'll bet that if you think hard you could identify at least one instance when you've experienced this dynamic at work. It often begins with a single instance when the team underperforms, but the results are rationalized as good in some way. Once the team sees that performance has become a subjective thing rather than one measured against hard metrics, rationalization for other subpar work often begins. It's not an effort to shirk hard work, it's simply the group's way of dealing with its fear about increased future expectations.

Some creatives struggle with this fear of success for their entire careers. They perpetually shrink back from challenges because they are afraid that they will end up "out of their league" or with more work on their plate than they can handle. While we have to be wise about the amount of work we choose to take on, we also must be willing to ignore these subtle and destructive impulses to "coast" and "go with the flow." If we don't stretch ourselves, we don't grow. Growth is uncomfortable, but without the discomfort our capacity doesn't remain the same, it shrinks. If we're not growing, we're dying. In the next several chapters you will learn some very practical (and manageable!) practices that will help you grow, let you practice taking risks in controlled environments, and cultivate the energy you need to face the ever-increasing expectations of your work.

> Growth is uncomfortable, but without the discomfort our capacity doesn't remain the same, it shrinks. If we're not growing, we're dying.

Fear of success is often more destructive than fear of failure because it's masked in the guise of wisdom. It sounds like our friend. It can feel like a mature attitude toward knowing your role, playing your part, and pacing yourself. But ultimately it will cause us to miss opportunities.

Question: **Are you withholding yourself creatively because you're afraid you can't sustain the pace of your success? Have you ever held an idea back because you were afraid of the consequences? Do you, in any way, feel "unworthy" of success in your life or career?**

EXPECTATION ESCALATION AND THE INHIBITING NATURE OF COMPARISON

The final assassin of creativity is expectation escalation. We allow comparisons to affect our current creative engagement. The moment we place concrete expectations on the end results of a project—this upgrade is going to double last year's sales figures!—we begin closing off potential executions and helpful thoughts because we deem them "not useful enough" in accomplishing our escalated expectations. Doing this too early in the creative process can seriously derail brilliant ideas and prevent them from ever seeing the light of day.

The result of all this is a phenomenon I call "expectation escalation." As our perceived expectations escalate, we become almost paralyzed with concern about not measuring up. We want our ideas to be fully formed from the beginning rather than giving our creative process time to play out. If we don't see the idea as stacking up against the best of the best, then we don't spend time on it. But this ignores the reality that all brilliant creative executions began as infant ideas and had to be tweaked and developed.

I've witnessed three sources of unhealthy expectations, and

each affects our creating in the same fundamental way. Expectation escalation causes us to self-limit as a result of comparison.

Our Past Work

Have you ever had difficulty getting started on an idea because you were afraid that it wouldn't measure up to something you'd previously done? Sometimes our expectations for our own work can get in the way of full creative engagement. It's unfortunate that we are often our own worst critic and that we often criticize and deconstruct our work well before it's ready.

You have a great idea and, at first, you're very excited. Soon, though, you begin to think back to previous work you've completed, comparing those final products with the seed you're currently nurturing. Even though your current work is still in its infancy and so of course can't stack up to a fully formed and executed idea, you're not willing to give yourself that grace period. Instead, you do a quick assessment of whether the work is worthwhile based on nothing more than these artificial expectations. As a result, you don't give the idea time to develop.

When you do this you fail to realize that (1) all your past work was once unformed and in midprocess, and that (2) you always remember past work more fondly than you actually felt about it at the time. In hindsight, recalling how a project succeeded is easy, but in midproject, there is always a lot of doubt and confusion involved. We tend to forget the angst and uncertainty we felt while doing the work and instead look only at the end results.

I don't mean to imply that all comparison is bad. There is both good and bad in playing this comparison game. You want to continue growing in your skills, and comparing your current work to past work can help benchmark your growth. But you don't want to fall into the trap of shrinking back from engagement simply because you're afraid of not measuring up. The key to using comparison effectively is to withhold it until later in the process.

When you are in the early stages of a project you need as many possibilities in front of you as possible. There are enough limitations in place thanks to your organization, your peers, and your client; you don't need to limit yourself, too.

Question: **Do you find yourself frequently putting past work on a pedestal? Do you think that this limits your current ability to creatively engage in any way?**

> **There are enough limitations in place thanks to your organization, your peers, and your client; you don't need to limit yourself, too.**

Our Managers and Peers

In the same way that we can experience escalated expectations for our work based upon our own past work, we can be tempted to artificially escalate the expectations of our managers and peers when they are not communicated clearly. Because of the already complex nature of creative work, and the time-versus-value tension discussed in the previous chapter, a lack of clarity around organizational expectations will sometimes result in our going overboard in our work as we try to cover our bases. But this means that we often do extra and unnecessary work, and waste energy that could have been more effectively applied to the creative problems at hand.

Question: **Do you have an accurate understanding of what's expected from you by the organization? By your coworkers? When was the last time you had an "expectations" conversation with your manager?**

Our Heroes and Competition

I love to read industry trade magazines and blogs. They can be a wonderful source of inspiration and information about what's happening in the wide world of business. But they can lead to a sinister side effect: it's very easy to let the work of others paralyze us.

This is a real problem in the design world. I've spoken with many designers and creative directors who feel the constant pressure to measure up to the work they are seeing on the covers of industry magazines. Some companies will cut these pieces out and hang them on the wall as a form of inspiration to the team, but these displays can sometimes feel more like a "why can't you be more like your older brother?" talk from your parents.

While you certainly need to be willing to learn from the competition and from our own creative heroes, don't let their influences cause you to condemn your own abilities. In his book *Free Play*, improvisational violinist Stephen Nachmanovitch writes, "It's great to sit on the shoulders of giants, but don't let the giants sit on your shoulders. There's no room for their legs to dangle!"

In other words, there is a form of oppression that emerges when we allow the work of our influences or competitors to drive our creating in an unhealthy way. The creative process is a personal assault on the beachhead of apathy and a push to explore and break new ground, even when we are uncertain of a successful result. The more we try to force a successful (and derivative) result, the less likely we are to see true breakthrough. It's only when we are free to abandon our need to measure up and instead simply trust our abilities that we will begin to see real creative brilliance emerge.

"It's great to sit on the shoulders of giants, but don't let the giants sit on your shoulders. There's no room for their legs to dangle!"

—Stephen Nachmanovitch

Question: **Are you in the habit of comparing your current work with the finished work of your heroes? Does that affect which ideas you are willing to explore or cause you to condemn your abilities?**

Tim Senff, director of ReachOut at Crossroads Church in Cincinnati, regularly leads trips for people to travel to other continents to participate in service projects. Some of these trips draw hundreds of participants. Tim finds that rigid expectations stand in the way of a good experience for these groups. His advice to participants? "We want to be expectant, but without expectations." In other words, expect that great things are going to happen, but don't place parameters on what those things will be; inevitably, they will lead to disappointment or cause you to miss opportunities simply because you're not looking for them.

I think this is a wonderful description of what a healthy and productive creative process looks like. We want to be expectant without expectations. We want to be able to engage in the creative process without requiring concrete results too early. When we do this, we neutralize the effects of unhealthy expectations and allow ourselves the full freedom that is required in order to take creative risks and see our infant ideas to completion.

> **The creative process requires that we be expectant without expectations.**

While dealing with the specter of expectation escalation within an organization can be difficult, doing so is critical to doing your best work. Concrete objectives and a clear path to completion are key, but you need to be careful to suspend your judgment until later in the project. You can't become paralyzed by other people, by your past work, or by an unclear understanding of organizational expectations. Any one of these can cause you to perform at less than your best.

The assassins of the creative process will creep up on us and invade our life. It's possible to spend days, weeks, or years trying to recover the clarity and passion we once had for our work. The only way to counteract them is to establish practices in our life to

THE SIDE EFFECTS

keep us focused and engaged. That's where we're headed in the next section.

THE PRACTICES

We often reject ideas that seem too simple or too obvious out of hand. If something is simple, the thinking goes, it must be ineffective. But the greatest performers across a wide spectrum of fields understand that the most basic and fundamental practices ultimately lay the foundation for brilliant results.

Vince Lombardi was unarguably one of the greatest coaches in NFL history. As each new season began, he would gather his team together on the first day of practice for his opening pep talk. In the circle were NFL legends, such as Paul Hornung, Bart Starr, and Jim Taylor, as well as numerous other veterans and returning Super Bowl winners. As the players leaned in to hear the great coach's opening words, Lombardi would begin his pep talk by thrusting a ball into the air, declaring, "Gentlemen, this is a football!"

How insulting! These players were some of the greats of the game! They had accomplished more in their time than many of today's top players would hope to accomplish in their entire careers. Why not begin by talking about the offense, or about why last season was so successful, or about the strategy for their first game?

Coach Lombardi understood that the foundation of every great work is a solid grasp of the fundamentals. He was sending a message to his team that no matter how great their accomplishments, and no matter how talented they are, the only path to consistent, long-term success is to maintain focus on the basics as the foundation for everything you do.

Though the framework for how we look at them is unique, some of the practices we'll discuss in upcoming chapters have been implemented by many creatives to great success for centuries. My goal is simply to help you establish them and find a foundation of stability and rhythm that will allow you to experience creative accidents in your everyday life. Remember that common sense is not common practice, and that people who succeed are often those who do the little, everyday things that others won't.

PART

CREATIVE RHYTHM

FOCUS:
ZEROING IN ON
WHAT'S CRITICAL

 4. **If you want to thrive in the create-on-demand world,** you must develop the capacity to focus deeply. Though broad and shallow engagement may feel necessary because of the number of priorities on your plate, to be truly effective you must cultivate the ability to do quick, focused dives into the depths of a project and emerge with useful ideas. More important, this must be done in spite of the increasing pressure to do things faster, better, and cheaper.

Because we tend to gravitate toward possibilities, many creative people wrestle with focus. We can quickly become fascinated with new ideas or bounce from unsolved problem to unsolved problem without really solving any of them.

This "priority ping-pong" prevents us from engaging in the kind of deeply focused thinking that facilitates insight and moves the needle on our projects. As the number of unresolved creative problems in our work increases, we can become overwhelmed or generally discouraged by all that's left undone.

> "Where observation is concerned, chance favors the prepared mind."
>
> —Louis Pasteur

The only solution is to stop living reactively and to instill a new practice for thinking deeply about your work: lock in on the heart of the problem quickly (define), establish your game plan to center your activities around the most crucial priorities (refine), and organize your work so that you're minimizing distractions and staying on course (cluster). Developing these practices will increase the number and quality of spontaneous insights you experience.

Two key factors, which largely stem from dissonance, affect our capacity to focus: unhealthy assumptions and the "ping."

UNHEALTHY ASSUMPTIONS

A few years ago my family visited Lake Erie for a long Fourth of July holiday. As evening approached, we were preparing to walk to the pier to watch the fireworks when our five-year-old middle son started getting nervous. We explained that fireworks are fun and that there was no reason to be afraid, but he was having none of it. We finally persuaded him to make the trek to the lake, but he protested all the way. When we arrived at the perfect vantage point and began setting up our blankets, his protests grew frantic.

"Owen," I said, "fireworks are perfectly safe. They're not going to fall on you."

"I'm not worried about them falling on me," Owen replied. "Fireworks make my feet fuzzy."

"They make your feet fuzzy?" I replied, puzzled.

"Yes. Like at Disney World."

We had taken a vacation to Disney World the previous year,

and because his short legs prevented him from keeping up, Owen had ridden my shoulders around the park. At one point an unexpected plume of fireworks startled him. At the time, he had been sitting on my shoulders for an hour or so, and his legs had fallen asleep. Shaken out of his reverie by the fireworks, he realized that he had lost all feeling in his feet. His four-year-old mind assumed that it was the fireworks that had made his feet "fuzzy."

For more than a year, I realized, Owen had carried this assumption with him and had lived in terror of feet-zapping fireworks. I was eventually able to convince him that fireworks have absolutely nothing to do with what he felt in his feet when he was on my shoulders, but to this day he is still a little nervous around them.

What my son experienced is something we must guard against in our creative work. Our minds are excellent at solving problems and forming patterns. It's the primary reason we're able to survive past the age of two. We learn from our experiences, and some of those lessons keep us from making mistakes that could significantly harm us, like touching a hot stove or punching someone bigger than us. But this ability to connect the dots can also cause us to adopt false assumptions about cause and effect.

For example, it's easy to assume that because something has always been done a certain way, that must be the one and only right way to do it. We sometimes develop the assumption that because a system or method brought us success in one instance, it will always do so. Or we may assume that because something didn't work in one instance, it will never work under any circumstances. Any of these assumptions can, over time, be disastrous to our creative process because they limit how we look at problems.

A theory advocated by brain scientist and founder of Palm Computing Jeff Hawkins in his book *On Intelligence* contends that our minds function by constantly predicting what will happen next and then comparing these predictions with what we actually experience. In doing so we develop patterns that make our future predictions more accurate, a library of experiences against which we can validate new information. This allows us to make many decisions in our life quickly, often based upon hunches and with very little information.

> **Assumptions can be disastrous to our creative process because they limit how we look at problems.**

While this capacity is helpful in allowing us to assimilate new information and experiences quickly and usefully, it can also mire us in mental ruts that prevent us from seeing opportunities that are obvious to others. Instead, we see only the world through the lens of our assumptions, whether they're true or false. False assumptions can limit the options we have at our disposal as we attempt to generate ideas.

Any good statistician differentiates between causality and correlation. There's a critical difference between "these two things happened at the same time" and "this thing caused that thing to happen." But this distinction is often lost in the hustle and urgency of our daily activities. We're often so busy that we fall into habits that prevent us from focusing on the real issues or that cause us to ignore opportunities simply because we're not looking for them.

Because the method by which ideas emerge often seems beyond our control, the temptation to develop rituals around behaviors that have proven successful in the past is real. For example, if we had a creative breakthrough in a meeting attended by a certain group, we might establish a standing meeting with those people. If visiting a certain website yielded inspiration for a project, the site becomes our go-to source of inspiration for all projects that follow. We develop systems to replicate our past successes—or to prevent replicating our past failures—but all we really do is fossilize these processes and create rigidity in our life.

One manager I encountered had developed a ritual for getting to work very early in the morning as a way to get a head start on the day. This practice was remarkably effective for a while, but over time his productivity in these times began to wane significantly. His solution? Get up earlier! Get to work sooner! But this didn't improve his performance. After a brief discussion, I was able to convince him that his incredible productivity during those initial early morning sessions had little to do with the mechanics of his schedule but was more the result of what the change in routine did for his focus. What began as a means for getting an early start on his truly important work had turned into nothing more than additional time to check e-mail, shuffle papers, and work his task list. We established a few objectives for his morning time, including what he should and should not do, and soon he was back to his highly productive ways.

It's possible to go for days, weeks, or months at a time drifting through our schedules, attending meetings, and going about our work without ever stopping to think about whether any of these activities are really beneficial to the work. While effective boundaries can be useful in helping us gain focus (as we'll discuss shortly), false boundaries based upon assumptions can actually cause us to use our energy ineffectively and distract us from what we're really trying to do.

My family lives in a home that backs up to a nature preserve. A few years ago, when we were doing some remodeling, we decided to build a home office on the back of our house as a place for me to read, think, and write. I greatly enjoy the view of the woods and the animals that frequently walk past my window. (With the exception of the coyote pack. We want them to leave. Now, please.)

One of the unfortunate annoyances of living close to nature is that insects find their way into our home from time to time.

About a year ago, I was nestling in for some morning reading on the sofa in my office when I saw a wolf spider sidle up through the gap between the cushions.

I despise spiders more than just about anything else in the world. After ushering him into the spider afterlife, I practically took the office apart looking for any of his eight-legged colleagues before resuming my morning study routine.

Here's the thing: every single morning thereafter, I inspected the cushions for unwanted guests. That's 1 minute per day for 365 days, or about 6 hours a year of wasted energy trying to prevent something that hadn't happened since. I developed a permanent system to protect against something that had happened once. (I've since realized the error of my ways and stopped the ritual.) This was significantly misplaced focus and energy based on a one-time negative experience.

In the same way, we may misplace our creative energy because of false assumptions that are based upon one-time experiences—either successes or failures. I once coached a writer about some significant life and career changes she was planning to make. Over the course of several sessions, we kept coming back to the issue of her lifestyle and her need to generate enough income to maintain her standard of living.

As I prodded her to question whether her multiple residences and all her other expenses were really indispensable, she came to realize that many of her life decisions over the past several years had been based upon the assumption that her lifestyle and spending habits were nonnegotiable. This assumption led to a kind of creative stasis, because she was able to take on only work that would pay well enough for her to maintain her lifestyle, and as a result she had little time available to take on the kind of work she loved. She had lived with a self-limiting false assumption, and the result was that many excellent options weren't even on the table as she planned her career. Over time this had devolved into creative block, career confusion, and procrastination. Once she was able to break through these assumptions, she was able to see how she had many more options than she'd originally thought and found new energy in her work.

When you allow false assumptions to creep into your life, you become inflexible, less capable of focusing on the issues at hand. The key to overcoming them, as we will explore shortly, is to effectively define the creative problems you're really trying to solve.

Question: **Are there assumptions you're making about your current projects that are artificially limiting your options? These could be the result of what's worked or failed in the past, something your manager once said in a meeting, or the way in which you're trying to avoid the worst-case scenario. Take a few minutes to list assumptions that may have crept in and are causing you to lose traction or do less-than-optimal work.**

THE "PING"

We live in an age of unprecedented access to information. If we want to know something, we can gain access to that knowledge within a few keystrokes. I'm old enough to remember the days when doing a research project meant hopping in the car and making the trip to the library to crack open the encyclopedias or to (God forbid!) attempt to find something on microfiche. Many people under twenty years old have never had to leave their homes to gain the information they need. With the ubiquity of cheap Internet access, a world of information is now at our fingertips. While technology is the great equalizer with regard to information and communication, there are also some unique new pressures that accompany its newfound place at the center of our life and work.

Technology is an extension of our capacity to accomplish our will. If we desire to do something, technology can help us do it cheaper and faster. But not all the things we want are necessarily beneficial to us. We are often willing to sacrifice long-term gain for the sake of a little short-term satisfaction, and for many of us this tendency is seriously affecting our capacity to focus and be present in the moment. We have almost limitless options at our disposal to cure even the slightest case of boredom. It's human nature to crave entertainment, and if that's our will, then technology serves it very well. Entertainment doesn't necessarily mean games or movies; it can be anything that gives us a charge or provides some kind of distraction from our work, even e-mail or random web surfing. More than ever, we have the capacity to live in a state of perpetual entertainment.

A few years ago I noticed a disturbing pattern in my life. It was a tiny sensation, a little pinprick in my gut every so often. I called it the "Ping." The Ping is that little sensation that occasionally prompts me to check my e-mail or my social media accounts. It's the impulse to mindlessly surf news sites instead of doing something productive. And as my number of options grew (turns out there *is* an app for that), the pull of the Ping became ever more powerful.

The Ping wants to be my master. It wants to own me. It wants me to serve it. The Ping even has a life philosophy for me: "Something out there is more important that whatever is right here."

If a meeting gets even the slightest bit boring, I reach into my pocket to check my e-mail. If I have a few minutes in line at the store, I check my feeds on Google Reader. Rather than being heads up and actually paying attention to what's happening in front of me, the Ping tells me, "Hey, you don't have to be bored. You have options."

The net result? It's more and more difficult for me to be fully in one place, to focus on what's in front of me. I'm losing the capacity to think deeply about whatever I'm experiencing because I tend to gravitate to whatever feeds the Ping. I default to whatever will entertain me right now. Neil Postman's 1985 work *Amusing Ourselves to Death* is more relevant than ever in the era in which we are fiber-optically wired to our every desire. Postman argued that our obsession with television is ruining our culture's capacity to think and engage in important societal issues. But now, with smartphones, netbooks, and tablet devices connected 24/7 to anything and everything we could want, we have unprecedented capacity to be in a state of perpetual distraction.

Our work demands make it difficult to be in one place at a time. We feel the weight of our overflowing inbox, or we need to break away in the middle of writing a presentation in order to check the text message that just came in on our phone. But in order to do our best work, we need to learn to pay attention to what's in front of us and to develop the capacity to stay focused on our objectives. The Ping slowly eats away at our effectiveness.

> **In order to do our best work, we need to learn to pay attention to what's in front of us and to develop the capacity to stay focused on our objectives.**

Author Linda Stone coined a term for the way many of us are living: "*continuous partial attention.*" We're always kind of here, and kind of somewhere else. (We've had to pass laws to prevent people from text messaging while driving with their knees at 65 miles per hour!) This divided focus prevents us from bringing our full energy and skill to the work we're doing. Some of us slip in and out of zombielike engagement with our work as we scan the horizon for something more appealing to feed on. Can we really do our best work this way?

Productivity blogger Merlin Mann calculated that if on average we work an 8-hour day, 50 weeks per year, and check our e-mail every 5 minutes—just to see if anything is there—we check our e-mail 24,000 times per year. That's not responding to e-mails, and that's not doing anything about what's actually in the e-mails. That's not even thinking about the contents of the e-mails. That's just checking to see if the little mail icon is bouncing in our dock.

Let's take this a little further. Let's say that each time you check your e-mail—just glance down at that little icon—it takes you 10 seconds to do so and then regain your focus on what you were working on before the Ping stole your focus. (That's pretty conservative, given that many experts would say that it takes anywhere from 30 seconds to 3 minutes to regain concentration after even a momentary interruption.) This means that over the course of the year you spend 66.6 hours just checking to see if there's anything that would be more stimulating than what you're doing right now.

What could you do with 67 hours per year of focused, concentrated time? Do you think you could get something done? Do you think you could get moving on a project or generate a few business-changing ideas?

When we allow the Ping to rule our life, we allow it to rob us. And we don't even notice it happening because the Ping is robbing us of our focus 10 seconds at a time. Fortunately, the right practices can refine our focus and keep us deeply engaged in our work for longer stretches of time. You don't need to get rid of technology; you just need to use it in a way that increases your capacity to do what matters to you. You need to set priorities and home in on them rather than living in a state of continuous partial attention. You can't do your best and most insightful work when you allow the Ping to rule your life.

Question: **Where do you find the Ping at work in your life? Do you find it difficult to maintain your focus on what's in front of you because you're always scanning the horizon for something more entertaining? List a few ways you think you could mitigate this in your life. Some methods might include occasionally (and strategically) leaving your smartphone at home, logging in to your e-mail only at predefined times, or setting aside specific times for entertainment so that you don't feel entitled to occasionally zone out in the middle of times when you need to be deeply focused. (If something makes you feel a little nervous just thinking about it, that means you're probably on the right track.)**

DRIFTERS, DRIVERS, AND DEVELOPERS

As you strive to gain focus, there are three modes you can fall into in your work. In order to work effectively you must broaden your focus enough to allow you to see potential connections, but not so much that everything seems random and you are unable to gain traction.

A Drifter is someone who does whatever work they feel like from moment to moment. In this mode, a creative floats from objective to objective and task to task without really thinking about how any of them connect. You might be answering e-mails one minute, writing a few words on a proposal the next, and then making a phone call or two. Your work is fragmented. While you might get things done, there's no overarching sense of purpose behind how you approach your work, and you don't really have a prescribed plan for how you will get things done.

To the Drifter, finishing a project feels a lot like pushing a wall forward because you have no priorities—your efforts and attention are spread thin across everything you need to do. You waste effort on task switching and may have a difficult time deciding what to do next. This is not to say that you're not productive; Drifters can accomplish quite a lot. But your approach is so scattershot that you aren't able to leverage critical opportunities. While no one wants to think of themselves this way, many of us stumble into Drifter behavior from time to time.

When we realize that we're drifting, we sometimes overreact and slip into the second mode: the Driver. This is when you become very focused on outcomes. From the moment you receive an objective, you map out a workflow, break the larger goal into tasks and subtasks, and structure your work schedule in order to get it done as efficiently as possible. You become driven by checking tasks off lists and probably carry tons of data around just in case it will come in handy.

Drivers have a very strong sense of what they're trying to do, and they typically follow a prescribed system for accomplishing their work. But in their effort to drive to the end objective, they often overlook or discount opportunities. Drivers have a narrow-focus horizon. They are too microscopically focused on the objective (as they saw it from the beginning) and are often reluctant to redirect their energy when new opportunities emerge in the course of their work. They're simply too busy trying to get through the project to respond to new insights that—they fear— could lure them off track.

The third, and most desirable, mode is the Developer. Developers have a strong sense of the overall objective and have a sense of purpose and priorities in navigating there, but instead of just plowing through the work with their noses down, they purposefully approach each task or element of a project as an opportunity to develop new connections or potential ideas.

Developers are world makers. They are able to take a lot of disparate-seeming elements in their work and weave them together into something useful because they are not too hyper-focused to recognize the patterns around them. They have cultivated the skills necessary to focus intensely for a period of time, then release their focus in order to assess the lay of the land. This allows them to iterate rapidly and quickly redirect their efforts. They also treat their work activities like investments. They are trying to maximize return rather than simply get through the work as efficiently as possible.

The more you can cultivate a Developer mind-set, the more likely you are to experience unexpected creative insights that move a project forward. Developers lock in on the heart of the problem quickly (define), establish their game plan and center their activities around their most crucial priorities (refine), and organize their work so that they're minimizing distractions and staying on course (cluster). However, unlike the Driver, they are able to occasionally take a few steps back and redirect their efforts as needed rather than simply following their predefined plan. For the remainder of this chapter we will look at a few practices that will help you cultivate a Developer mind-set.

DEFINE: USING CHALLENGES TO LOCK IN ON THE PROBLEM

Despite the lip service that managers pay to the importance of setting good objectives, I frequently encounter creatives and teams who are unclear about what they're trying to accomplish. While the general direction of a project may be apparent, the specific objectives are significantly less than clear. For example, many managers will throw out meaningless objectives such as "increasing our client's market share" or "refreshing the brand identity" without giving concrete examples of what that means in practice. As a result, many creatives have to not only solve the problems posed by the project itself but also overcome the dissonance stemming from a total lack of clarity. Much of this churning and confusion happens on a subconscious level, and it's a waste of creative brainpower that could be harnessed to more effective ends.

Inventor Charles F. Kettering famously said that "a problem well-stated is a problem half-solved." We can spend a lot of time spinning our wheels if we're not clear about what we're really trying to do. There's a difference between having a sense of where the project is headed and truly understanding the objectives, and this is where many of us go off the rails. We may know enough about a project to get moving on it, but we never really stop to think deeply about what we're trying to accomplish and how we'll know when we're done. So we set off in a vague direction fueled by vague objectives. This often means that we waste valuable time and energy trying to gain clarity later in the project or course correcting when it's much more expensive and stressful to do so.

I once had a conversation with a designer about the importance of setting good rails in his creating. He shared with me that he had simply lost his passion for his work and that he felt like much of what he was doing was simply rehashing old ideas over and over. I asked him if he had ever taken the time to write out objectives for his projects, and he replied that he'd never thought to do it. I continued to probe and asked him if he'd ever thought to write objectives for his personal life. Again, the answer was no, but I could see that our conversation was unlocking something for him.

After some time, I checked back to see how things were progressing. It was as if something had unlocked in him simply because he'd taken the time to write down clear objectives for his projects and for other areas of his life.

Having experienced painful, late-project course corrections many times, I can comfortably say that the most important work of a project happens at the very beginning.

In any project, there is the main problem we're trying to solve, but there are also many subproblems. One effective way to gain traction quickly is by positioning project objectives in the form of questions designed to surround the problem. We call this establishing "Challenges."

When I sit in on client brainstorming sessions, I'm surprised by how often the stated objective is obscured by complex language or corporate jargon. While the lingo might impress upper management or reflect the latest overhyped buzzwords from business gurus, they only make it harder to solve the problem we're facing by obscuring the discussion.

When we phrase our objectives simply and in the form of a question, we lead our minds directly to solving the problem. For example, when the Accidental Creative team was developing Idea Traction, our online collaboration tool for teams, we divided the project into several Challenges:

- What are the key functions teams need to collaborate online?
- How do we enable remote creative direction for leaders?
- How can team members share inspiration for projects?
- How can team members most effectively share opinions and collaborate around ideas?
- How do we give leaders a quick look at their team's progress?

The common approach would be to write "Idea Traction" on a whiteboard and say, "OK . . . anyone have any ideas?" Because we defined the problem with clear, specific questions, we could focus our thinking, thoroughly explore the problem, and analyze aspects we would surely have missed otherwise.

One of a leader's most critical roles is to identify the Challenges for each project. Setting out four to six Challenge questions for each project will help the team surround the problem and ensure that all critical aspects are given adequate attention. The more quickly you can focus your mind on what you're *really* trying to do, the faster you gain creative traction.

If you're like most creatives, you're probably currently juggling several work projects, each of which is at different levels of priority and completion, and you probably also have many personal projects you'd like to get moving on at some point in the near future. When there are this many priorities on our plate, it can be difficult to zero in on what's really important as the swirling complexity causes us to lose our sense of focus. In addition, bridging the gap between a project's stated objectives and our daily work is often difficult. By dividing each project into four to six Challenges, you allow your mind to do what it does best— identify useful patterns.

The more quickly you can focus your mind on what you're *really* trying to do, the faster you gain creative traction.

FOCUS

Make a habit of blocking off about thirty minutes at the beginning of a project to clarify your objectives and establish Challenges. List each project that you are currently working on. Under each project's name, list four or six questions identifying problems to solve in order to complete the project successfully. For example, you're charged with developing and releasing a product called "X":

▶ **PROJECT: "X"**

CHALLENGES:

- What is the unique functionality of "X"?
- What would make "X" appealing to twentysomethings?
- How can our messaging differentiate "X" in the marketplace?
- How can we keep production costs for "X" low?

Before, you may have seen "X" as a giant mess of issues and problems to solve, with no clear sense of priority or purpose. With these Challenges, you give yourself permission to home in on one problem at a time. You're also able to identify new opportunities as you recognize patterns between your responses to various Challenges that you wouldn't have otherwise seen. For example, your exploration of how to make "X" more appealing to twentysomethings ("communicate authentically and transparently") may give you insight into a unique functionality "X" needs to possess ("create a feature that shows total cost of use over time"). Your life becomes a series of concrete problems to be solved rather than a series of vague concepts ("guard the brand identity," "increase market share," "make new employees feel welcome") that you're responsible for. This helps you stay attuned to potentially useful ideas throughout the course of your day because you are focused on specifics rather than generalities.

This practice is also effective for personal projects and career and life planning. You can use the practice of establishing Challenges to identify opportunities in your life and to help you work more effectively on personal creative projects. (We'll talk more later about how to use Challenges to pull all of the practices together and get moving on what matters most.)

REFINE: THE BIG 3

On my office whiteboard you will see "The Big 3" followed by a short list of my current creative priorities. The Big 3 refers to the three things I need to gain creative traction on right now. They aren't necessarily my biggest projects, though they often are. Rather, the Big 3 is best described as the three most important "open loops" in my life and work. They are the three most important items that I'm still looking for critical insight on.

The Big 3 is a constant reminder of where I need to dedicate my creative bandwidth. While I may have other projects on my plate, the list is a reminder of the more important creative problems that are still outstanding. When I read a book, I'm looking for connections or concepts that are relevant to my Big 3. When I have a conversation, I check it against my Big 3 for possible new insights. When I watch a movie, I'm on the hunt for anything relevant to my top priorities (while, hopefully, enjoying the flick). When I meet someone new, I stay open to how they may be able to help me with my Big 3.

Many times I've glanced at the Big 3 and five minutes later had a conceptual breakthrough simply because my creative priorities were top of mind. If they hadn't been, I may have missed those insights because I wasn't looking for them.

Your mind is a wonderful servant but a terrible master. If you don't refine your creative priorities on a regular basis and focus in on a few things at a time, your mind will go into a full retreat, and you will become overwhelmed with all that's left undone. By choosing what you're going to focus on, you're relieving your mind of the pressure to resolve every creative problem simultaneously. You are giving yourself permission to lock in on only three problems at a time rather than the dozen or more that may be on your plate.

This also applies to a team context. Clarifying the top creative problems yet to be solved helps the team know where to put its energy and eliminates the guesswork often required to establish priorities. One of the greatest gifts any creative leader can give to their team is to regularly refine focus by utilizing the practice of establishing the Big 3.

It's important to note that the Big 3 is not necessarily determined by level of urgency. Some items are urgent but are chugging along fine and don't require top-of-mind focus; others may have a long horizon but require traction sooner rather than later in order to do your best work. A few things to keep in mind:

- The Big 3 is not a to-do list. In other words, it's not the place where you put your urgent daily items or overdue projects. It's the place for your open conceptual loops, projects where you're still looking for a key insight, like the name of a new product or a new marketing strategy.
- The Big 3 is not a wish list. You don't put your lifelong dreams and vague ambitions on it. It's a practical tool to help you focus on your current work.
- The Big 3 is not your project list. There will always be other things you're working on. This is just intended to be a way of prompting your mind about your most important creative priorities right now so that they're top of mind to help you identify potential connections.

How to Establish Your Big 3

Begin by listing all the projects in your life, both work and personal. (There is no difference between the two—if something is on your mind, it's on your mind.) Then go through the list, asking yourself which require some kind of conceptual breakthrough in order to move forward? Which are in stasis until you set the strategy? These are your candidates for the Big 3.

Of the remaining candidates, which three are most pressing? Which weigh the heaviest on your mind, keep you up at night, or incite the most conversations among the members of the team?

Keep the list in front of you as much as possible. I've developed the habit of writing my Big 3 on an index card and keeping it in my notebook or in my pocket. As I mentioned before, I also write them prominently on the whiteboard in my office as a reminder of the projects that are still missing a creative breakthrough. Seeing my Big 3 on a regular basis reminds me of what's most critical right now and helps me to filter the stimuli I take in each day through the lens of my most important creative priorities.

One member of our online coaching community, AC Engage, relayed that simply having her Big 3 regularly in front of her had markedly increased her productivity. "From this practice alone I was able to double the number of children's book illustrations I did in the six months before—just because the Big 3 was always in front of me." We've found that the refined sense of priority that accompanies the use of the Big 3 frequently yields this kind of productivity boost.

No one else needs to know about your Big 3, even if you are using it to help you lead an organization. I introduced one manager to this practice, and he has been using it effectively for quite some time to clarify his team's creative priorities, even though no one on the team is aware his Big 3 list exists. He relayed that it's brought a great amount of clarity to his team's process because his increased focus has trickled down into his conversations with team members.

Once you experience a key insight that you were looking for with a project, you can remove the item from the list and add something else. It's also possible that something will come along and become a higher priority before you've achieved your insight.

That's fine as well. There are no hard-and-fast rules for this; it's not intended to be a task list or a Project Queue. It's simply one effective way to keep the conceptual hurdles we still need to jump squarely in front of us as we go throughout our day. It's a lens through which to process the world. This sets us up for unexpected insights and creative breakthroughs.

CLUSTER: CHUNKING SIMILAR TASKS

There is a practice in retail management known as "intelligent adjacency." It means placing complementary items next to each other, like toothbrushes and toothpaste, so that when a customer finds one item, the proximity of the complementary item makes it more likely they'll buy both.

Many of us reflexively place items according to intelligent adjacency all the time in our own lives as well. We place items in convenient proximity to one another in our workspace and in our homes in order to save time or energy in some way. As I sit here typing, most of the tools I would need for working on this chapter are within my reach, such as my research, pens, notebooks, index cards, and a stapler. I make sure that I don't waste time getting up and walking across the room each time I need to take a note or check something. It's natural for us to think about basic usability when it comes to our physical surroundings, but how often do we think about how conveniently our workflow is structured? Have you ever considered clustering work projects that require similar kinds of thought into the same blocks of time? Many of us don't do this, with the result being that we waste precious focus shifting gears between different kinds of tasks. For example, we may spend all day on e-mail, jumping in and out of our inbox or even checking e-mail while we're in the middle of doing some other kind of work. But each of these little mental breaks causes us to lose creative traction and can ultimately add up to less than optimal work.

The practice of clustering is about finding intelligent adjacencies within your work and clustering your efforts to keep you engaged and focused more deeply and for longer periods of time. By doing this you minimize the psychological cost of switching tasks and constantly having to refocus your efforts.

There are several benefits to clustering your work:

▶ LIMITING FOCUS SHIFTS

Each time you break from what you're doing to focus on something else, you lose traction, and regaining it takes more time than you may think. If you cluster similar kinds of work into blocks of time dedicated to the work, the penalty for these focus shifts is minimized. For example, clustering all your e-mail into one session, or several sessions broken up throughout your day, prevents the focus shift that occurs each time you leave your creative work to see what's in your inbox.

▶ UNEXPECTED BREAKTHROUGHS

As you cluster similar work you will begin to notice reoccurring patterns and areas of potential overlap. You may also find that there are similar issues you're facing on different projects that stem from the same source. As a result, clustering can lead to conceptual breakthroughs. For example, a discarded idea for one project may be perfectly appropriate for another, or research that you're doing for one client may yield an unexpected insight for another client. These breakthroughs may never have occurred if your workflow was fragmented rather than clustered.

▶ IMPROVED FLOW

Because you are focusing for longer periods on similar work, you will experience a greater sense of immersion in the work, making it more likely to have a breakthrough (and more likely you'll enjoy the work). You can dive deeper with an oxygen tank than if you have to resurface every few minutes for air. The net result is that you will spend more concentrated time thinking deeply about the problems you are facing and will be more likely to get to the brilliant ideas that often take time to emerge.

Here are some ways I've seen clients apply this practice to great effect:

- Set aside an hour in your day to do strategic thinking and plan your projects. It's much easier to maintain a conceptual, strategic mode of thinking than it is to try to regain it once you've switched over to more concrete tasks.

- Cluster meetings as much as possible, and make sure to leave large blocks of uninterrupted time open each week. People tend to spread their meetings throughout the day, with fifteen minutes to a half hour between them. This practically eliminates your ability to engage in deep thought. To immerse yourself in a problem requires stretches of time, and if you're allowing for only small pockets of time to think creatively, you're probably wrapping up just when you're getting to a place where you're likely to start experiencing insights. In addition, you may want to schedule your strategic thinking time ahead of meetings if possible to avoid the energy lag that often happens in their wake, and so that you'll have time to think ahead about the issues you'll be discussing.

- Set aside a dedicated time each day for responding to e-mail. Rather than living perpetually in the inbox, cluster all your communication in dedicated blocks of time. This will help you focus more deeply throughout the day rather than being constantly interrupted by the demands of others. If you need to do frequent e-mail checks throughout the day, that's fine, too. You can schedule ten minutes at the beginning of each hour to address your inbox. While there are certainly exceptions, there are very few e-mails that will cause our world to come crashing down if not addressed within an hour.

- The same advice goes for phone calls and face-to-face encounters. Whenever possible, try to clump these together so that you avoid the energy drain required to gear up for and gear down from personal interactions.

- Separate your conceptual/creative time from your concrete/task time. When you fragment your day with fifteen minutes of design or writing, ten minutes of invoicing and time tracking, five minutes of e-mail, et cetera, you are paying a significant task-switching penalty. Try to give yourself—as much as you are able—no less than a half hour of uninterrupted time whenever you are doing design, writing, or other largely conceptual work, and an hour is preferable. If the projects don't require that much time, try to cluster a few together. Not only will this help you stay focused longer, you will also regain a significant amount of time wasted by switching programs, moving windows around on your screen, and quickly checking that funny little headline that caught your eye.

This is not an exhaustive list, and I'm certain that there are many other opportunities you can see for how to cluster your own work. Regardless of the level of flexibility in your schedule, there are always small ways you can more effectively structure your work so that you're minimizing task-switching cost.

Gaining focus and quickly establishing a game plan gives us a significant advantage in our creative work. The better we become

FOCUS

at weeding out irrelevant information and staying alert for potential insights, the more likely we are to experience creative breakthroughs. Similarly, the better we are at defining and refining the problems we're trying to solve, the more likely our minds will do what they do best—identify potentially useful insights.

RELATIONSHIPS: BEING BRILLIANT TOGETHER

 **Creative work isolates you because a substantial** amount of it must be accomplished alone. But your relationships with others are some of your most valuable creative resources. If you neglect these relationships, you are starving yourself of a substantial and potentially game-changing influence on your creative work. When you neglect your relationships, you limit yourself to your own experiences. But when you approach your relationships with purpose, you will be able to draw on many lifetimes' worth of experience for insight and inspiration.

Many of us don't think much about whom we invite into our lives or how we manage those relationships. Instead we treat the connections we form with others as something that happens naturally as a matter of circumstance or convenience. Coworkers and family are the only people many busy creatives take the time to connect with. And though they love their families and like their coworkers, this can quickly lead to a situation where relationships feel more like obligations than anything else. Our relationships will eventually grow stale unless we are diligent about directing and cultivating them.

Investing in healthy, thriving relationships yields long-term benefits for everyone involved and can be especially beneficial in allowing you to see the world from new perspectives, exposing you to unexpected creative insights and helping you stay inspired.

In his book *Where Good Ideas Come From*, Steven Johnson states that many of the brilliant and innovative ideas throughout history have resulted from networks of creative people sharing, collaborating, and challenging one another to explore the *adjacent possible*. He says, "The trick to having good ideas is not to sit around in glorious isolation and try to think big thoughts. The trick is to get more parts on the table." Johnson says that a key way to get more parts on the table is to put yourself in networks of other creatives who are striving for the same thing. He continues, "What kind of environment creates good ideas? The simplest way to answer it is this: innovative environments are better at helping their inhabitants explore the adjacent possible, because they expose a wide and diverse sample of spare parts— mechanical or conceptual—and they encourage novel ways of recombining those parts." We can put ourselves in these kinds of environments—and experience creative accidents more consistently—by being purposeful about how we cultivate the relationships in our lives.

The key to cultivating creatively stimulating relationships is threefold: you need relationships in your life in which you can be real, you need relationships in your life in which you can learn to risk, and you need relationships in your life in which you can learn to submit to the wisdom of others.

CREATIVES AND INTROVERSION

The workplace demands a lot of us. We are frequently balancing the demands of multiple personalities (sometimes within the same coworker), processing various communications, and dealing with difficult conversations. Navigating all this can take a toll on our mental and emotional reserves.

It's not a rule by any means, but many creatively gifted people tend to display a natural tendency toward introversion. Perhaps the isolated nature of a lot of creative work is what calls many of us to our chosen profession to begin with. We love to get lost in the process of moving big conceptual rocks and developing exciting and elaborate new systems, strategies, and ventures. Due to this natural tendency toward introversion, collaboration and dealing with others throughout the day can drain our batteries pretty quickly.

Introversion doesn't mean that we don't like being around people; it simply means that we derive our energy from being alone rather than from being around others. We may prefer to curl up with a good book after a period of intense interpersonal interaction, or find a quiet conference room to do our work in peace. These are important and effective methods for recovery, but the slippery slope of introversion for the creative is that we may isolate ourselves more than we should. We sometimes begin to see the act of maintaining a relationship as an obligation that pulls us away from our important work, rather than as an opportunity to stretch ourselves, explore new possibilities, and take advantage of collaborative opportunities within our team. If we want to thrive over the long term, we must reclaim the power of relationships in our life and establish practices that help us leverage the gifts and accountability that only thriving relationships can provide.

INTIMACY AND GENEROSITY

Keith Ferrazzi, author of *Never Eat Alone* and *Who's Got Your Back*, believes that relationships are the key to success, enhancing our ability to thrive over the long term in our life and career. As he explained to me, there are two critical elements of any successful relationship: intimacy and generosity.

Intimacy is when we regularly share our life with others, and they in turn share their lives with us. By allowing another into the inner circle of your life, you not only give them the opportunity to learn from your experiences, you also learn how to better communicate those experiences to others. Relationships are messy because they force us out of our comfort zone, but they also help us see problems and opportunities from a new perspective. When we invite others into our life, when we allow ourselves to be intimate, we quickly come to realize that there is an entire sphere of experience that we miss when we live in a silo.

> **"Anyone can sympathize with the sufferings of a friend, but it requires a very fine nature to sympathize with a friend's success."**
>
> **—Oscar Wilde**

The other crucial element of successful relationships is generosity. The creative process is an inherently generous act. Whether we are developing a strategy or crafting a piece of art, creating is primarily about sharing our insights and perspectives with others.

My friend Jeni Herberger has a theory about the nature of generosity and relationships. Jeni posits that there are two types of people in the world: those who live to fill other people's buckets and those who are always looking to get their own bucket filled. For the latter, even the act of complimenting someone else is an inherently selfish act because they are somehow secretly trying to take credit for the other person's work. When they offer up, "Hey!

Great job on executing that idea! It's a lot like something I did last year. Did I ever tell you about it?" it contains a subtle pat on their own back. They're looking to fill their own bucket.

But there are other people who derive their energy from filling other people's buckets. They love the thrill of seeing other people come alive, of collaborating, of giving away their ideas and subsequently the credit they deserve. They recognize that more ideas will always come, but investing in relationships and maintaining an ethic of generosity yields results we can't gain when we hold tightly and selfishly to what we think we deserve. These are the people others flock to and who invigorate an entire room with their creative energy. They thrive because they make it their mission to help others to thrive. I agree with Jeni— these people are the meaning makers, and in my experience they eventually come out on top because everyone wants to work with, and for, them.

When we obsess over getting our own buckets filled, we not only find ourselves disappointed with the results, we also regularly disappoint everyone around us. Our best creative work comes from a mind-set of abundance and generosity rather than one of scarcity. When we clamor for credit and fight over resources we perceive to be scarce, it infiltrates every area of our life and work.

> **When we obsess over getting our own buckets filled, we not only find ourselves disappointed with the results, we also regularly disappoint everyone around us.**

THREE STRATEGIES TO ENRICH RELATIONSHIPS

There are three strategies that can help you be more purposeful about your relationships. Each is designed to help you achieve more interdependence, inspiration, and accountability in your work. We are not wired to do life alone; the more we can network ourselves with others, the better. In his book *The Neuroscience of Human Relations*, professor and clinical psychologist Louis Cozolino says that "without mutually stimulating interactions, people and neurons wither and die." In other words, we need others as much as they need us. He continues, "From birth until death, each of us needs others who seek us out, show interest in discovering who we are, and help us feel safe. Thus, understanding the brain requires knowledge of the healthy, living brain within a community of other brains: Relationships are our natural habit."

Relationships give us perspective on our unique strengths, on which of our ideas are most likely to gain traction, and on how we can most benefit the world around us. Our relationships play a vital role in helping us understand how we can get moving on, and devote our best effort to, the work that really matters.

Start a Circle

Many of the greatest creatives throughout history have gathered in small groups to stay focused and engaged, and the practice continues to benefit those who go to the effort to instill it. It's something that I've done for years, and it's been an immeasurable source of inspiration and accountability for the work that I'm doing. These small group meetings can stoke your passion, help you stay aligned with what matters most, inspire and give you new ideas or directions for projects, and simply feed you emotionally in ways you may be lacking.

The size of the ideal circle varies. Some people prefer a smaller circle for the increased level of intimacy it provides, while others prefer to have a larger group in order to leverage a greater diversity of thought and experience. While the composition of your circle can vary, you want to invite people whom you believe you will have the ability to connect with in a meaningful way and who also want to do better creative work. Examples of circles that I've seen work very well include the following:

- A circle of aspiring entrepreneurs who gather to discuss their work, share tips on what seems to be working, and provide much-needed encouragement to one another. There is one such, called Continuous Web, that was a source of encouragement and even helped me find a few collaborators for early projects I was launching.
- A circle of visual artists who gather to share their latest creations and discuss their ideas. Artists often struggle to find good feedback for their work, and I've frequently seen artists go into especially productive periods upon finding a circle of likeminded peers to bounce things off of.
- A circle of creative pros who gather to talk about the pressures they're facing in their professional life and to talk about productivity tips and cultural trends they're noticing.

These are just a few examples. I'm certain that you can think of a few types of circles that could benefit your work. Though they are designed to be social gatherings, these circles facilitate the sharing of insights; they aren't just about getting together for drinks and a chat.

If you are organizing a circle, you should invite members you think will inspire you with their vision, their strategic thinking, and their track record of executing great ideas. Your group can gather anywhere, of course, but ideally choose a place offering quiet and privacy—the back corner of a coffee shop, someone's deck, a small studio space, a living room. You're looking for a place that affords space, comfort, and intimacy. (If you are looking for a tool to help you find other likeminded people, we've created a way on our website to form a circle with other creative pros in your city. For more information, visit AccidentalCreative.com/circles.)

Your circle get-together will revolve around each member answering three questions. In the first few meetings, someone in the group should play moderator, but as your circle grows more comfortable, there will be less need for directed conversation, and gatherings will likely flow much more smoothly. Here are the three questions:

▶ WHAT ARE YOU WORKING ON?

In other words, with regard to your work, what is at the top of your mind right now? The answer to this question will give everyone in the group a sense of the scope and nature of the work each is presently charged with. It also provides context for the rest of the conversation and may yield relevant creative insights from the group. Granted, there are always certain confidential matters that can't be discussed outside work, but it's usually possible to speak in generalities to get at the heart of the creative problem.

This question doesn't apply only to our on-demand work. These small groups are a great place to find inspiration for our personal projects. We should also share initiatives related to our passions and hobbies because it's a great way to gain accountability and creative traction on them. If you have a personal creative project that you've been toying with, or something that you've wanted to do for a while but aren't sure how to approach, your small group time is a fantastic way to get motivation and ideas for first steps.

Sometimes others can give you perspective on projects or show you potential solutions that you've overlooked. You may have blind spots due to a strangling degree of complexity or because you're simply too immersed in the work to see the obvious. Simply describing your work and the challenges you're facing to others who aren't immersed in the same level of intricate detail can often offer obvious new paths to explore.

> Sometimes others can give you perspective on projects or show you potential solutions that you've overlooked.

In his book *A Whack on the Side of the Head,* Roger von Oech shares a proverbial story about a Native American medicine man. Whenever the tribe was having difficulty finding new game, he would take a dried animal skin, crinkle it until deep lines appeared, then mark it with some reference points to orient them. He would tell the hunting party that this was an ancient tribal hunting map, and that the crinkled lines were the ancient game trails. Armed with this new map, the hunting party would set out on a new expedition, which, surprisingly, would lead to an abundant capture of game.

The map was nothing but randomly created lines on a dried animal skin—why did it lead the hunters to success? The answer is that it forced them to look in places they had unknowingly left unexplored. It got them out of their rut. This is just like the power of community when it comes to your creating. Your circle can give you perspectives and insights that are akin to the lines on a crumpled animal hide, pushing you to look in places you may otherwise miss.

▶ WHAT IS INSPIRING YOU?

This second question is valuable in any conversation, but it can be transformative in a small group. I find it incredibly enlightening to hear what is inspiring the hearts and minds of those I admire; this question is the one that generates the most additions to my list of items to read or experience, because each time I ask it I end up with at least a few (or a few dozen!) books, magazine articles, or movies to experience.

When you explore inspiration in the context of community, you get not only to see what influences the creative decisions of others but also to explore the mechanics of how others bring their inspiration to life. This can be valuable in helping you find new methods of approaching your own work and in ensuring that you're not falling into overly familiar and stale patterns. It's always encouraging to hear the stories of those who are getting things done. It kindles the fire we feel for our own work. There are many times when I've been itching to get out of a group meeting just so I can go home and get started on an idea that arose as a result of the conversation.

Often you will hear someone acknowledge that they read a particular book and then applied some of their newfound knowledge to a project. This is a powerful reminder that the best work we accomplish is frequently a result of being inspired by someone else. You shouldn't be ashamed of drawing inspiration from other sources and applying them to your own work. At the heart of it, that's the crux of innovation. Innovation is the collective grasp for "next," and it's always built on the work of those who went before. At the same time, you should have some ground rules in your circle that there will be an overall respect for the ideas of others, and that it's a safe place to share newborn ideas without the fear that they'll be hijacked by someone else. Group accountability can be a powerful motivator to keep everyone honest, especially in circles where there are only loose previous relationships.

> Innovation is the collective grasp for "next," and it's always built on the work of those who went before.

▶ WHAT WOULD YOU LIKE PROMPTING ON?

This final question is designed to help you cultivate group accountability for the work you're doing. It's likely that each member of the circle has a few projects that they want to get moving on but can't seem to find the requisite time or energy. Having a small group around to occasionally poke and prod us into action can be a really helpful tool to that end.

It's a good practice to end each small group session with a check-in on the projects that need action. These can be anything from an unwritten novel to an undeveloped business plan, but it should be something that you know you'd like to do and would like the group to help you stay focused on. Keep it simple, choosing one project that the group members will ask you about whenever they see you.

"Hey—how's that business plan coming?"

"How are your new designs developing?"

"Have you written the chapter outline for your novel yet?"

When you have specific accountability it gets you moving on the things that may otherwise continue to sit on your back burner. Once you discuss an idea with others, it's a lot more difficult to remain at a standstill. You feel the pressure to do something about it because you know you're going to have to give a report of your progress next time.

For example, one aspiring writer I met with was concerned that he wasn't producing good enough work and that he was instead just cranking out drivel. As a result, he found that he wasn't writing as often as he should have been, in spite of my advice to write no less than a thousand words per day, every day.

When I confronted him about his lack of consistent writing, he expressed that he didn't feel that his writing was good enough to be shared with others. "It doesn't have to be," I replied. "You just need to write until you come to the end of yourself—your fear, your anxiety, your inhibitions. When you do, there may be two hundred words that are good enough to share. That's fine. Job done. But you still have to write every day." Having this kind of accountability in his life has helped him stay on track and grow as a writer.

It's likely that some critics in your group will shy away from this kind of accountability. They'll say they don't need the additional pressure. They'll even tell you that the work itself suffers when subjected to this kind of pestering.

What you're hearing is a rationalization. These kinds of remarks are rooted in the critic's own fear of being held accountable to produce something, not in a genuine concern for the quality of the work. It's far better to have a mediocre outline of a novel or business plan that can be reworked later than a vague and flittering concept that is likely to fade away from sheer inertia. By acting, we make things concrete; action breeds motivation, not the other way around. We will often find inspiration only upon our first awkward attempt at progress. Having a small group to prompt you and hold you accountable to those first hesitant steps is like having a parent there to hold your hand when you're learning to walk as a toddler. It makes the risk more bearable knowing that other people are on the journey with you.

Be realistic in asking for accountability from the group, however. "I want to secure round-one funding for my start-up" might not be a reasonable first milestone, but "I want to sketch out a business model for my new boutique" is perfectly reasonable. It's important for the group to call out a member who is being unrealistic in their goals and timing. This is part of the group dynamic that will serve everyone and help the group achieve its collective aspirations.

Your circle could possibly be the biggest catalyst on your journey to experiencing regular and brilliant insights. Of all of the practices in this book, I'd encourage you to take this one most seriously. The sooner you leverage the power of interdependence, the sooner you will gain traction on the things that matter to you.

Head-to-Heads

We rise to the level of our competition. Athletes frequently talk about the importance of competitors who challenge them to push beyond to new levels of accomplishment. The same sentiments are often shared by business leaders and media personalities. Television personality Diane Sawyer is said to have remarked, "Competition is easier to accept if you realize it is not an act of oppression or abrasion—I've worked with my best friends in direct competition." We need others in our life to help us stretch and grow. We need to be challenged.

When you play one-on-one in basketball, you are competing head-to-head with another person. The same applies to running—many runners have experienced the benefit of having someone else alongside them to help them keep the pace. Simply knowing that slacking off means letting the other person down causes us to push ourselves to the limit and beyond. In essence, this kind of competition is not with the other person, but with yourself.

But what about your creative life? Do you have anyone in your life who is helping you keep pace and stay on a trajectory of creative growth? One way to cultivate the benefits of friendly competition in your creative life is to establish the practice of head-to-heads.

In a head-to-head meeting, two people get together, and each party is responsible for sharing new insights and new resources they've encountered since the last meeting. The discussion can be on any topic—a book you're reading, a seminar you attended, something you made—but the idea is to share something that will be both intriguing and challenging to the other person and that will stimulate discussion. In some ways, the head-to-head provides accountability for you to maintain regular times of study and purposeful experience because you know that you will be required to share something you've done since the previous meeting.

I have multiple people in my life with whom I've practiced these head-to-heads. One of them, Keith, is a neuroscientist, and though both our jobs require us to travel, we try as often as possible to get together to share our latest insights about creativity, science, and the brain. I have had numerous eureka moments sitting on Keith's porch as we shared what we were learning from the latest book we'd read, the latest research paper we'd seen, or the latest conversations we'd had with others in our network.

Many of our conversations have been formative in how I understand the creative process and have helped me significantly in my day-to-day work.

Here are some principles for effective head-to-heads:

1. **Set a time and be consistent.** Agree to a date, time, meeting place, and frequency for the meetings with the other person. Choose someplace quiet and comfortable, and make it a priority on your calendar. Once a month is a good frequency because it leaves enough time between meetings for each of you to have experienced something new to share and to have generated a few fresh insights that would make for interesting conversation.

2. **Vary your subject matter.** Don't harp on about the same topic month after month. The idea is to challenge each other with new insights and to spark conversation about things that may otherwise never show up on the other person's radar.

3. **Choose someone you respect and admire.** Preferably someone within your area of expertise. This will enhance the conversation when you get together, leading to ideas and insights more appropriate to each person's context. Ask yourself, "If I could see inside of anyone's notebook right now, just to see what they're currently thinking, who would it be?"

4. **Prepare about fifteen minutes of content.** Don't just show up with a sandwich. Spend time putting together materials to discuss. Build them around a topic or insight that you are presently working on or just fascinated by. Again, choose a topic of potential interest to both of you.

What subjects should you address? That depends on you and your creative goals. Here are some questions that may help you determine appropriate topics: What are you currently interested in or curious about? What have you read or experienced recently that you think the other person knows very little about? What new insights or thoughts have you had that are ripe for application? These are all good topics for your head-to-head time.

The idea behind these head-to-heads is to challenge and stimulate yourself with new thoughts and insights that could be useful in your life and work. Give your best to these relationships and you will get the most out of them. The best relationships are ones in which there is give and take, when both parties feel a sense of respect and admiration for the other. We want to root for the other person's success even as we are competing against them to share the best or most thought-provoking insights.

Establish a Core Team

Do you have others in your life who help shape your decisions and career choices? That sounds like a strange question, right? We don't like to think about the subject of authority because we are wired, and often told in many ways from our youth, that we need to question anyone in a position of power. This is unfortunate, because when we discount and distrust others in this way, we miss out on some of the key blessings that accompany putting ourselves in a position of learning and submission to others. We also lose the opportunity to allow others to help us navigate through difficult waters.

In his book *The Culture Code*, psychologist and consultant Clotaire Rappaille argues that this deep bias toward rebellion is still at the heart of American culture and behavior.

"The cultural reasons for this seem to be twofold," argues Rappaille. "Partly it's because we are an adolescent culture with an adolescent attitude. We don't want people telling us what to do and holding us to their standards. We want to discover things and learn how to do things our own way."

It's true that many of us like to do things our own way, making our own rules and following our own course. Many of the cultural icons we celebrate are "self-made" people who have achieved great things against the odds and without the help of others. These stories help us believe that we can, in fact, accomplish our goals if we persist over time. But sometimes these stories also reinforce a misperception that to submit to authority or to closely follow the advice of others, especially when it goes against our instincts, is a form of weakness. Contrary to this cultural belief, to remain humble and curious and to bend our life to the advice of those further along the journey is actually a sign of strength.

My children are currently studying the martial art Tae Kwon Do, and it strikes a special chord in my heart each time I hear them respond to their instructor with a hearty "Yes, Sir!" This sharp sign of respect tells me that they clearly understand who is the boss and that they are there to learn, not to lead. They couldn't gain anything from the class if they weren't willing to trust and submit to the greater experience and wisdom of Mr. Lewis, their instructor.

Is there anyone in your life to whom you bend your life and choices, someone in front of whom you take the posture of student? Some of us think that our student days end when we leave school, but many of the most accomplished professionals have maintained this posture of lifelong learning at the feet of others. Some call this mentoring, but I'm often concerned that this word doesn't communicate the weight of the other person's role in my life. I'm not just there to learn some interesting tips and tricks, some of which I may apply and some not. I am there to submit to wisdom and practical advice from someone who is a little further down the path and much more likely to see things that I'm currently blind to.

I give quite a bit of latitude to certain people in my life to speak truth to me. Sometimes it stings, but the temporary sting of unwanted truth is much easier to bear than the harsh sting that comes after a prolonged period of living in a world of imagined invulnerability. I would much rather have friends inflict these wounds than cynics, critics, or competitors, all of whom want me to fail.

There are three people in my life who have full permission to speak anything they want to me and whom I regularly meet with in order to review my goals and my progress. I consider them my core team, and they are always my first e-mail when something good happens or when I need advice. (In fact, when I was offered the deal for this book, my first instinct was to send an e-mail to share the news with them. Even though I was inclined to accept it, I wasn't going to make a move until the people I respect the most in my life had weighed in on the decision.)

Many of us have blind spots, especially as it relates to our creating. We will never be the most objective judges of our own work, and we will always have difficulty weighing big life decisions without bias. It helps to have people you respect and admire to shine light into dark places and help you see angles of a problem that you may otherwise have overlooked.

Whom can you trust to speak the truth to you, no matter how hard it may be? Whom do you trust to say the things that no one else will say? You must have these people in your life if you want to continue improving in your work.

> **Whom can you trust to speak the truth to you, no matter how hard it may be? Whom do you trust to say the things that no one else will say?**

It's critical to choose your core team wisely. You want people who have significant experience in areas where you may be lacking, and with whom you have a degree of personal rapport. You also want people who are likely to be vested in your success and who are willing to spend time to help you achieve your goals.

Right now you may be asking, "So how does this help me with my creative work?" We discussed earlier the importance of focus in gaining creative traction. When you have others in your life with more experience and a larger perspective, you can gain focus

RELATIONSHIPS

more quickly and get moving on what really matters. By learning from their experiences, you can avoid some of the mistakes that they made in their lives and careers. Having a core team in your life will help you prune your options and avoid the paralysis that often accompanies having too many choices in life. It's much easier to redirect once you are moving, but often you may not move at all if you are overwhelmed with options. You sometimes need other, more experienced friends to help you focus on the right data points.

Here are a few tips with regard to meeting with members of your core team:

If you are meeting for breakfast, coffee, or drinks, you should always pick up the bill. There are people in my core team who make much (much!) more money than I do, but I always pay any expenses related to our meeting. Why? Because I need to remind myself, and them, that I see this as an investment in myself and in our relationship. By picking up the check I am ensuring that I maintain the mind-set that my core team's time is valuable and that my time with them is an investment.

Choose people outside your company. You want to feel the freedom to speak whatever may be on your mind, and if your core team member is in the chain of command where you work, you will always be tempted to soften your comments. You may also be unwilling or uncomfortable sharing thoughts about leaving the company or dealing with your current manager. You need to have complete freedom in these conversations to bring up your most pressing issues, regardless of the subject matter.

Choose visionaries. At least one member of your core team should be someone who is a dreamer or a visionary. You want the kind of person who makes others nervous with the intensity and scope of his ideas. You want at least one person who will push you and challenge you to think uncomfortable and challenging thoughts.

Choose people from a variety of industries. Whoever is on your core team, make sure that they are a fairly diverse group with varied experiences. It's important to maintain a balanced diet of input from others. Advice from diverse perspectives will build a more solid foundation for your decision-making process. You are also much more likely to hear about new and interesting stimuli that may otherwise never show up on your radar. Consider your core team to be your personal board of directors. They are there to help you sort through important decisions and also to challenge and stimulate your thinking. You should choose these people as carefully as a public company would choose its own board. There is nothing more critical to your success than the people you surround yourself with.

Question: **What are some issues you need help sorting through right now? How may a core team be able to help you process through these issues?**

Your relationships provide the stability and clarity you need to do your best work, and they are also the key to staying emotionally engaged. For creatives, slipping into an overly conceptual mode and ignoring your emotional intuitions, or simply becoming emotionally numb to your environment, is a very real danger. Maintaining deep, vibrant relationships is a way to stay emotionally engaged, in tune with your environment, and poised.

Additionally, surrounding yourself with bright, motivated people will challenge you regularly to step up your own game. It is inspirational to hear what others are doing and to redirect some of their energy into your own work. It's also very motivating to be that source of inspiration and energy to others. When you give of yourself and are generous with others, filling their buckets, you will often find that you leave with more insight and energy than you came into the interaction with.

I realize that it can be challenging to apply each of these practices immediately. In fact, you probably want to start with forming a circle of likeminded creatives. Once you do, this circle can form the candidate pool for your head-to-heads and perhaps even your core team. At the very least, your circle will likely be able to introduce you to potential core team members in their own network.

Take your relationships seriously and treat them with purpose. You will be rewarded many times over.

ENERGY:
YOUR INVISIBLE ALLY

6.

As I write this, the midwestern United States is digging out from "Snowmageddon," as dubbed by the media. We have experienced snowfall unlike any we've seen in several years, and though my children love the sledding and canceled school days, for us grown-ups the snow means frequent shoveling and aching backs.

I have noticed two distinct strategies employed by my neighbors to deal with the snow. Some cleared it away a little at a time, shoveling a bit, allowing a few inches to accumulate, shoveling again, and so on. They opted for regular shoveling intervals with less effort required for each snow-clearing session. Other neighbors, however, would wait for the snow to stop, then clear it away a foot at a time. This approach required less continual effort and time, but the trade-off is that it required an all-at-once Herculean effort to clear the mountains of drifting snow.

For many of us, our workload feels a little like clearing snow in the middle of a snowstorm. Work continues to "fall," and we are under constant pressure to determine how we are going to handle it. Are we going to pace ourselves, moving all our projects forward an inch at a time, just to stay ahead of the pileup, or are we going to alternate sprints of extreme exertion, punctuated by pause? Do we expend ourselves in one heroic effort, or do we parcel out our heroism over time?

Unfortunately, we often don't have this choice because we're living in one very long, unending Snowmageddon of work. As the work continues to pile on, we have to expend tremendous effort just to stay ahead of it, let alone to develop any kind of effective strategy for completing it. Given the pace many creatives keep, the key to regular insight is to be strategic not only about the work we're doing but also about how we're doing it. According to recent key research, the solution may rest in how well we learn to manage our energy. In this chapter, I will share some specific practices that can help you stay engaged and energized when your creative work demands your best.

Imagine the perfect device, one that is maximally efficient and does precisely what it's supposed to do with the smallest effort imaginable. It is truly a marvel of engineering. Unfortunately, no matter how well designed the system is, it is useless without energy—no energy, nothing happens.

Every system requires energy to function. Whether it's a plant turning sunlight into sugar or your car burning gas on your daily commute, nothing functions without energy. But many of us overlook this fundamental law of nature when it comes to our creative work. Because the energy we expend shaping ideas is invisible, we fail to realize that there is a very real cost associated with every project we take on and every mental commitment we make.

Our brains are wonderfully efficient systems, but they require energy to forge ideas, memories, and thoughts—tremendous amounts of energy, actually. Although the brain is only about 2 percent of our body weight, it consumes about 20 percent of available oxygen and glucose. This means that when we are tired, our mind is less capable of functioning at its maximum potential. We are less likely in these times to forge connections and experience conceptual breakthroughs simply because our brain doesn't have the basic energy required to perform the complex tasks required to generate ideas.

In his book *How to Be Excellent at Anything*, Tony Schwartz argues that energy management is at least as critical to success as time management:

"The real issue is not the number of hours we sit behind a desk but the energy we bring to the work we do and the value we generate as a result," he writes. "A growing body of research suggests that we're most productive when we move between periods of high focus and intermittent rest. Instead, we live in a gray zone, constantly juggling activities but rarely fully engaging in any of them—or fully disengaging from any of them. The consequence is that we settle for a pale version of the possible."

What Schwartz articulates so well is that even if we effectively manage our time and resources, but neglect our energy level, our effectiveness will decrease over time. Today's success begets tomorrow's success, so for the creative worker, when you lack the energy to generate ideas today, it takes a toll on tomorrow's creative effectiveness. The longer the energy drain continues, the more you dig yourself into a hole.

I've spoken with many creative leaders over the years who have felt this dynamic in a significant way. One man, a successful consultant who spent years building an innovative boutique consultancy, had simply lost all desire to generate new ideas for his business. In our conversation he told me that he was in a rut, but as I probed deeper I discovered that this rut was really just an aversion to innovating that stemmed primarily from his lack of energy management. Over time he had grown weary of being the sole standard-bearer for his organization (and its chief innovator) because he recognized that any idea he generated was going to fall onto his shoulders to execute. As a result, he unconsciously avoided forming creative solutions to problems because he knew deep down that he lacked the energy to see the idea through.

Because he had not been careful in choosing new initiatives and managing his own energy and expectations over a period of several years, he had dug a hole for himself and his organization. And as time passed, imagining a way out of the hole became more and more difficult for him, because any new potentially business-saving ideas would be his responsibility to implement. It seemed nearly impossible to generate any kind of momentum for the business.

Energy management is critical to staying out of ruts. Like a gambler who falls behind and needs to wager bigger and bigger amounts to get back to even, the creative in the risky habit of ignoring energy puts himself in a seemingly impossible situation. But it's never too late to build healthy practices around energy management. We can start making wise choices now about how and where we spend our energy to ensure that we're not neglecting the important things in our life for the sake of what's convenient. As productivity guru David Allen says, "Mosquitoes ruin the hunt for big game." It's all too easy to waste the energy we need for important creative objectives on unproductive or unfocused behaviors.

> **Like a gambler who falls behind and needs to wager bigger and bigger amounts to get back to even, the creative in the risky habit of ignoring energy puts himself in a seemingly impossible situation.**

ISN'T ENERGY "RENEWABLE"?

Few of us think much about how our energy level affects our ability to create. Energy consumption is more difficult to measure than time management and other markers of productivity. Also, our energy is a renewable resource, so many of us believe that it is perfectly acceptable to race through our week until we crash, spend the weekend recovering, then start the cycle all over again.

But this mind-set is deceptive. Creative work requires that we stay ahead of our work. Tomorrow's ideas are the result of today's intentions. When you rely on a "just-in-time" workflow, you will quickly find it difficult to do quality work—and you'll also find yourself lacking the drive to do anything about it.

What happens at that point? Many of us panic. If ideas aren't flowing, we stare even more intently at the problem, pull late nights at the office, or pump ourselves full of caffeine in order to stay alert and hopefully shock our minds into generating something brilliant. This unhealthy cycle is the unfortunate reality for many creatives, and making the break from this type of lifestyle can be difficult. For some, this cycle is broken only when they lose their job or suffer some sort of mental or emotional breakdown. For others, it results in a helpless compromise, which could mean months or years of settling in and continuing to trudge along, cranking out mediocre work while feeling like they are betraying the best part of themselves. They have the energy to do only what they need to do in order to not get fired, but they have no excess energy for innovating or tackling personal creative projects.

This lifestyle and its effects on our creativity are cumulative. Creative insight is frequently the result of conceptual momentum, and the most difficult thing to do in the early stages of a project is to gain traction. Building momentum requires excess energy. When we lack the necessary energy, mobilizing around insights can be difficult. In fact, sometimes we overlook the small clues and stimuli that may yield insight because we simply lack the energy to pay attention to the nonessentials.

This is no way to live, especially when there's something we can do about it. While I don't believe that energy management alone is sufficient to set us up for creative brilliance, it is certainly the most neglected of the five areas of Creative Rhythm, and for many of us, energy management will require the most discipline if we want to change our habits and restructure our life in a healthy way. Striking the right balance when instilling practices around energy management will feel a little uncomfortable, perhaps even painful, at first. But experiencing the results of effective energy management makes these practices worth all the temporary discomfort.

> **"Creativity is a natural extension of our enthusiasm."**
> **—Earl Nightingale**

Rennata is a paralegal by day, as well as a wife and mother. She had always wanted to do something with her passion for art but couldn't seem to find the energy to do it because of the multiple roles she was juggling. After applying some of the practices explored in this chapter, she was able to find new resources to help her pursue her dream. In an e-mail to me, she wrote: "I have come to accept that creativity has a rhythm, what I tend to think of as an ebb and flow much like the tides." Rather than expecting to do everything at once, she began to put some practices into her life to help her consistently, and over time, work toward her goals with a keen eye on energy management. "I have found that by establishing the habits that support a creative individual, I was able to find the time that I never knew I had. I am now the manager of a co-op art gallery right across the road from the law office where I work."

Rennata's experience is one of many like this I've encountered in my work. Once creatives begin to put some structure around energy management, they often find that they have more energy and time available than they'd previously thought. It's often simply a matter of ensuring that their available resources are being funneled into the most effective places.

While there are many practices I could include here that relate to managing energy through a physically healthy lifestyle, such as adequate sleep, a healthy diet, and abstaining from harmful substances, I'm not going to directly address these, because there are plenty of books and articles on the subject.

(Here's the short version: eat a healthy and balanced diet,

including lean proteins and lots of vegetables, sleep seven to eight hours a night, steer away from too much caffeine and sugar to avoid the accompanying crashes, don't abuse alcohol, and no—other than pharmaceutical—drugs. For a comprehensive treatment on these suggestions, I recommend Tony Schwartz's comprehensive book *How to Be Excellent at Anything.* I've also listed additional articles and resources at AccidentalCreative.com/book.)

Instead, I am going to address two often overlooked but highly effective practices that can set you on the path to having enough energy to generate brilliant ideas.

WHOLE-LIFE PLANNING

Each and every second, we encounter millions of stimuli in our environment, but we are conscious of only a few at any given time. Right now you are likely feeling the weight of this book (or your e-reader) in your hands, the pressure of your chair on your rear, and the temperature of the air around you. But chances are you weren't thinking about any of these before I called them to your attention. That's because the only way you are able to survive as a human is by selectively ignoring stimuli that aren't immediately relevant.

Selective attention is incredibly beneficial to us in that it allows us to focus on what matters in a complex and dangerous world. But for creatives, this kind of behavior can also cause us to lose sight of the big picture, and what's really going on in the grand scheme of our life, for the sake of what's immediately urgent or pressing. Often we unconsciously compartmentalize data as relevant or irrelevant to the problem at hand, conceptually dividing our life into various "airtight" chambers that don't interact with one another. We like to think that the various areas of our life are like file folders that we can pull out of the cabinet, explore, then replace without affecting the other folders in the cabinet.

We examine the various areas of our life and work, make commitments on them, and generate ideas for them, in isolation.

To reinforce this, the preponderance of self-help literature over the past few decades has focused on effectiveness in various areas of our life. There are books on managing work, managing home life, and effectively managing time by dividing responsibilities into categories. But this kind of "divide and conquer" technique is destined to fail because it ignores the interconnectedness of all areas of our life and the effects that a commitment in one area has on another. We need to build the practice of occasionally stepping back to examine our life as a whole and establishing a rhythm around energy that accounts for all the commitments in our life. This will help us avoid the energy drains that zap our capacity for regular insight.

The Fallacy of Compartmentalization

Because we tend to divide our life into buckets, we talk about things like our "work life" and our "home life" as though we can somehow slip out of our skin and assume another identity when transitioning between them. But trying to compartmentalize the various parts of life can take a toll.

Every area of our life is hardwired to every other area. It is impossible to perform a task in one sphere and not have it affect another. Energy we put toward a work task is energy we can't put toward a personal project. Similarly, every personal commitment we make, even if it's just a commitment to think about something, requires energy that will not be available when it's time to focus on our work.

How does this affect our ability to generate ideas? When we are in a very busy time at work, one in which we're required to generate a lot of ideas in a short amount of time, we need tremendous amounts of energy and focus. But many of us make commitments and expend energy on other, less critical projects thoughtlessly during these times without considering the consequences. We don't realize that each commitment we make affects every other. We fail to plan ahead and take into account the creative energy that will be required by our work during a specific week and continue to make commitments, plan meetings, or allocate time to work on unrelated projects.

Most of us assume that as long as time is available, we can continue filling it up. This is how we have been trained to think about productivity—it's all about efficiency. But mindlessly stacking unrelated activities and projects into a week where we expect creative breakthroughs on important projects only drains our energy and fractures our focus. This goes for personal commitments, too. We will miss critical insights that could lead to conceptual breakthroughs simply because we are operating at less than optimum capacity. However, if we take into account the season we are in at work and at home, along with all the associated demands, we will be able to make commitments wisely rather than by instinct.

I've met and worked with many people who blow right past this principle at great cost. In fact, I used to be one of them. During one five-month period of my life, I was growing a creative team from five members to twenty-five, continuing to manage the daily demands of my very challenging fifty-to-sixty-hour-a-week job, dealing with the needs of our newborn second child (and his older brother), working on the adoption of our little girl from Guatemala, launching a nonprofit to fund international adoption and planning an associated benefit concert, working on a book with a colleague, working on the early stages of what has become Accidental Creative, performing with a band and writing music with my songwriter friends, and attempting to maintain some type of interpersonal health with my wife and close friends.

At the time, I remember feeling like I was being quite productive. I was accomplishing more than I ever had, seeing success across every area of my life, and feeling pretty good physically. Until I hit bottom. Hard. Because I technically had the time I needed to focus on each of these projects, I didn't think there was any problem with pursuing them with full guns blazing. I would stack hour after hour with project activity and creative demands, but unknowingly my creative engine was burning oil.

One day, I realized that though I was technically "working" on all of these projects, I was gradually becoming less effective in each of them. I stopped having ideas for the book I was working on, and I was straining my relationship with my coauthor. Team and organizational leadership priorities became fuzzy, and my team was suffering badly. Ideas weren't flowing for our most important initiatives. My interpersonal relationships, including with my wife, were strained. Most surprising of all, everything that I was once quite excited about felt like an obligation rather than an opportunity. I was spent. I was a shell of myself. I wasn't able to bring the best part of myself—my creative insights and leadership—to anything that mattered to me. I had to take time off from work just to reground myself in what I was really trying to do. I had to trim several initiatives out of my life—at the expense of the personal relationships involved—just to get my head above water. The worst part was that my family had been feeling the effects of my overextension for a very long time, and I'd not even noticed. My wife and I had to have some frank discussions about setting boundaries in my work, including the amount of hours I could put in.

The principle that I'd blown right past in my pursuit of creative invincibility was that each commitment I made, and each project I decided to take on, required something more of me than just my time. Each required my energy. And because I was not being strategic and purposeful about the number and nature of the simultaneous commitments I was making, I soon found myself in energy debt. I was creatively inverted and no longer had enough energy to generate the ideas I needed just to keep my head above water.

When you are planning your life, you need to account for every commitment you make in every area. This means that when you are in a busy season at work, you need to be disciplined enough to trim back the number of personal commitments you make. Similarly, when you are entering a busy season in your personal life, you need to be purposeful about the extra commitments you take on for work. While you can't always choose what you work on, you can be careful and strategic about where you focus your energy outside of those core commitments.

> **When you are planning your life, you need to account for every commitment you make in every area.**

Question: **Can you think of a time in your life when the convergence of your personal commitments and your work commitments have caused you to feel overwhelmed and ineffective?**

The Three Horizons of Whole-Life Planning

There are three horizons of whole-life planning that I recommend to clients: weekly, monthly, and quarterly. It is critical to get ahead of your energy commitments and examine them objectively. Saying no to a new opportunity is very difficult in the moment, but if you have been strategic in your planning and know what a new commitment will truly cost you, then you can refuse new opportunities with confidence. Once you understand your limits, you will be able to manage your energy more effectively. Remember, this is about setting yourself up to have conceptual breakthroughs in the areas of your life and work that matter most.

▶ WEEKLY

As part of your weekly checkpoint (which we'll discuss in chapter 9) analyze the demands of the coming week. As you look at your calendar, don't focus on work-related commitments alone. Remember, your personal commitments affect your energy just as much as your work ones do. (In fact, I'd strongly encourage you to keep only one calendar with both work and personal commitments in the same place, or use two calendars in the same place that can be selectively shown or hidden, such as in Google

Calendar. It's difficult to look at multiple calendars in multiple places and get a good sense for how overcommitted you really are. If you can't keep your personal and work commitments in the same calendar, at least have both calendars available as you do your weekly checkpoint.)

Pay attention to those activities that you find invigorating, such as meeting with clients, brainstorming sessions, or strategy sessions, versus those you find draining, such as follow-up calls, invoicing, or weekly status-update meetings. As much as you are able, try to space out the energy-draining activities throughout your days and week rather than stacking them together. If you have multiple difficult conversations on the agenda for the week, try not to put them back-to-back on your calendar, or you're guaranteed to be fairly useless the rest of the day. Instead, try to space them out and create buffers.

For example, if you have multiple draining phone calls to make back-to-back, try taking a short walk or spending five minutes with headphones on listening to music in between. While on the surface this may appear to be slacking, you are actually restoring your energy and making sure that you will be able to give your best effort to the next call. You can also apply this method to other draining back-to-back activities as a way to cleanse your palette and recuperate a bit before diving into your next exertion of energy.

Buffers, or quick energy-building activities, can also be helpful in managing energy as you shift between various roles throughout your week. One practice that I've effectively built into my life is to establish a buffer between work and home life so that I don't carry the angst and pressure of work home to my family. During my weekly planning time, if I see that I'm going to have an especially busy week, I plan to arrive at work fifteen to twenty minutes early so that I can leave early at the end of the day. With that extra end-of-day time, I will stop off at a bookstore and browse new titles. I find that this is a quick way of renewing energy and "rebooting" my system before interacting with my family.

When I fail to practice this and arrive at home still a bit

stressed from the day, I'm usually reminded by my son Owen, who has taken on the responsibility of announcing to the family, "Daddy's just a little grumpy tonight." That's not acceptable to me. I want my family to get my best. Buffers, whether between work and home or between energy-draining meetings, can be an effective way to reboot and ensure that you're always giving your best to whatever is in front of you. As you're planning your week, make sure that you're placing them strategically.

This is also where you will put all your energy-giving activities on the calendar and commit to them. When will you study, read, or experience other stimuli this week? When will you have time to yourself to strategize and generate ideas for your projects? When will you take a walk or exercise? What does your sleep schedule look like this week? Are there any late nights? If so, what does that mean about what should happen the next morning?

Again, in all these things we are not attempting to strike some kind of "life balance." We are simply being strategic about managing energy so that we have it when we need it to generate ideas. If we are wise in our energy management, we will find that ideas emerge when we least expect them. Our minds are constantly working in the background to solve whatever problems we give them. We just need to be strategic about clearing the way and ensuring they have the energy they need to do their job. It's amazing what happens when we work with, rather than against, the natural flow of the creative process.

▶ MONTHLY

During your monthly checkpoint (again, to be discussed later), you need to spend time analyzing what's on the horizon over the next several weeks. This is where you can make strategic choices about new projects, both work and personal, relationships you want to rekindle, and overall priorities in terms of energy use. If you see a new work project emerging and anticipate that it will require a lot of your time and energy, scaling down your expectations about personal commitments may be wise. (You will probably want to have this conversation with others in your life.) Similarly, if your month is looking a little light, then it may be time to take on a personal project that's been waiting in the queue.

This is also where you want to develop a template for your month. Are there specific practices that you want to build into your month as buffers? When will you perform the tasks that give you energy, like exercise, study, or connecting with friends? Setting expectations about these things on a monthly basis will help you make choices about where you will spend your energy so that you won't have to instinctively or reactively make them in the moment. Remember that creativity craves structure. When you establish effective boundaries, you are focusing your creative energy rather than allowing it to run rampant.

▶ QUARTERLY

During your quarterly checkpoint you will be looking at your life rhythm as a whole and establishing priorities. Are there significant milestones on the horizon that need to be accounted for? Are there important principles in your life that are being neglected and need to be revisited? Are there projects that you've always dreamed of pursuing but can never find the energy to get moving on? Now is the time to get these on paper and to start analyzing what can be done over the next quarter to initiate them. Again, your eye is primarily on energy management, so you are looking for opportunities to be strategic and wise about your life and which projects you pursue according to what will be required of you. You want to be poised to bring your best effort to all your projects, even the personal ones. If the upcoming quarter contains several new work initiatives, "build rocket-powered personal jet pack" might not be the best objective to initiate, but "write proposal for rocket-powered personal jet pack" may work.

This quarterly planning time is also when you want to get any new and intriguing work projects in the mix. Are there things that you've wanted to suggest or pursue but haven't because it's never a good time? See if there's any aspect of the idea that you could begin to implement this quarter.

Make certain that you're taking into account every upcoming commitment, milestone, and project. If there are especially busy seasons for your family (birthdays, anniversaries, et cetera), take those into account as you are setting expectations for the upcoming quarter.

Whole-life planning recognizes that your creative process is the result of the merging of all your experiences, skills, and passions. When you are able to strategically and purposefully structure your life so that you are giving your best energy to what's most critical, ideas will naturally start to flow in situations when you need them most. As mentioned, you will be learning more about how to integrate this practice with all the other practices in the chapter on checkpoints.

ELIMINATE LESS EFFECTIVE ACTIVITY

A second energy-management practice closely related to whole-life planning is pruning. We all live with the illusion that we can have it all. This illusion is sold to us in the media; we are bombarded by ads and the news with images of people who accomplish superhuman feats of work without sacrificing anything in the process. And it doesn't help that when we look around it seems like many people around us are living this "have it all" dream as well. They take a significant role at work, lead a few charitable initiatives, are active in their family life, and always seem to have a story about some weekend project they've been tinkering with on the side. If we're honest, encountering these people can make us feel like we're simply not pulling our weight as a human being.

Do you want to know how these people are capable of accomplishing so much? It's likely because (1) they are projecting an image of extreme productivity that doesn't match reality, (2) they are overextending themselves and are about to crash, or (3) they've learned the secret of energy management, and especially the practice of pruning. They are concentrating their energy and creative efforts on a select group of activities that provide them with the maximum amount of productivity. And because creative insight and productivity are cumulative, they continue to maintain forward momentum as long as they are mindful of their energy.

As mentioned above, each choice you make to do something is a choice *not* to do something else. I'm often reminded of something my father-in-law used to tell my wife when she was a child: "You can have anything you want, but you can't have everything you want." That's opportunity cost in a nutshell.

If you want to have the energy to creatively engage with the important things, you need to carefully choose your creative priorities. We each have a threshold for how many creative problems we can effectively manage at a given time. Taking on any additional obligations or commitments will decrease your overall effectiveness, and removing too many will mean you're settling for less than your full potential. You want to feel stretched but not overextended.

Knowing When to Reach for the Shears

In a good vineyard, the vine keeper is constantly pruning, but it's not that the pruned branches are dead or diseased in some way. Rather, the keeper removes young, unproductive branches so that much-needed nutrients can get to the older, fruit-bearing parts of the vine. If the young growth isn't pruned back, the vine will bear less fruit and eventually produce none at all.

Doesn't this seem strange? It's a bit counterintuitive to cut away healthy parts of a vine to increase its overall longevity and productivity, but this practice has been employed for centuries in vineyards around the world because it is effective.

This same principle of nature applies to the natural rhythms of your creative process. Every day there are little sprouts of growth that emerge in your life. New opportunities, new projects, new ways to expend our energy. Distractions. Temptations to divert our resources or attention. Many of these "sprouts" are very good things. But for some of us, these little opportunities continue to pile up until every crack of our life is full. Soon these very good but nonessential distractions are diverting our energy away from the tasks that are really crucial to our productivity and momentum. This is the beginning of a downward spiral of productivity, and it stems from a lack discipline around where we choose to expend energy.

> If the young growth isn't pruned back, the vine will bear less fruit and eventually produce none at all.

Pruning Can Be Painful

Beyond obvious time wasters, like excessive TV watching or Internet browsing, which can be pruned without too much of a struggle, some of the things we need to prune from our life are very good things. They are projects we enjoy, new ideas we are excited about, or relationships we would prefer to continue.

It can be difficult to eliminate things from your life that are giving you immediate joy and seem to be doing no harm. In fact, it can seem downright sadistic to deny yourself the pleasure of working on a project that you love and to which you can add unique value. But just as the young, fruit-bearing branches on a vine must be pruned back in order to provide needed resources to the critical sections of the whole plant, you must learn to identify the activities in your life that seem to be providing good results in the short run but will eventually decrease your effectiveness in the most critical areas of your life.

ENERGY

Many people don't realize how strangling the cumulative effect the semiproductive activities can have. Louis, a lifelong financial planner working to reinvent his career, went through one of our courses about establishing Creative Rhythm. A few months later he relayed that—after being painfully choosy about what to work on—he had already begun to see a lot of new opportunities emerging. "I've realized that this is really about the long term, like my whole life." While before Louis was a bit paralyzed because of the vast opportunities in front of him, after establishing some guidelines for how he would engage, he says that he found increased focus and experienced life-changing results. Once he chose to say no to some opportunities, others began to grow.

In many ways, you are defined by what you say no to. In design, they call this "negative space." It is the part of the composition or sculpture that contains nothing. This negative space is what balances a work of art and gives it visual continuity. Similarly, music is defined as much by the silence as by what is actually played. Without the spaces in between the sounds, music would be one deadening roar.

As you craft your life and make decisions about what to act on versus what to abstain from, you must recognize the importance of negative space in developing creative ideas. The time between your active moments is when ideas are formed, insights are gained, mental connections are forged. If your life is a constant blur of activity, focus, and obligation, you are likely to miss critical breakthroughs because you won't have the benefit of pacing and negative space. What's not there will impact your life as much or more than what is.

Identifying Your "Red Zone" Activities

In American football, the red zone is the area on each end of the field inside the twenty yard line. What happens in this area is a key determining factor in a team's success or failure. Teams that easily advance the ball down the field but can't score in the red zone will lose games. Teams that play great open-field defense but can't prevent scores in the red zone will lose. Performance within this very small sliver of the field often determines the overall success or failure of a team.

As you examine your life, and especially your creative work, it's important to be able to identify the red-zone activities that will really make a difference and generate forward momentum during the particular season you're in. Some qualities that mark red-zone activities are the following:

Activities that you can uniquely do or add value to because of your position or expertise and that move a project forward. While there are a lot of ways you could be spending your time, there are a certain number of activities that you are probably the best person for. Maybe it's because of your experience, or because you are the one most familiar with the situation, but there are certainly a few situations that are mostly dependent on you to move them forward.

Activities that increase your personal capacity to generate ideas, such as study, purposeful ideation, or intelligence gathering. These are typically the first activities to go during a busy season, but you must ensure that they find a place in your game plan. If you neglect them for too long, you will find your effectiveness decreasing across the spectrum of your life and work.

Activities that provide cohesion or creative traction for your team in such a way that it increases future capacity. For leaders, these activities include such things as regularly clarifying the objectives and organizational priorities, clearing obstacles for your team, or taking time to celebrate when the team experiences a success.

ENERGY

Activities that feed your energy, such as adequate sleep, exercise, or spiritual practice. While these should be obvious inclusions in every season, they are often significantly neglected during the busy times. But these are just the times when we need them the most. This is like a football team's deciding not to block because they're so close to the goal line. It's self-destructive to ignore the fundamentals when you are at your most busy and critical times professionally.

Your red-zone activities are likely to be made up of some combination of these qualities. Really pouring your energy into them not only increases your immediate productivity, but it also generates momentum in your life and work.

Similarly, it's important to identify the activities in your life that could be described as ineffective, unnecessary, or damaging to your overall productivity, and prune them out of your life. These can be time wasters, such as needless shopping, relentless gaming, and, as mentioned previously, excessive Internet browsing or TV watching, or they can be tasks that you're doing out of obligation, habit, or routine. It's not that these activities by themselves are bad or wrong, it's simply that each of these activities is taking the place of something that could be more effective in helping you generate ideas or move your work forward.

Getting Started with Pruning

Pruning is best practiced in your monthly and quarterly checkpoints. You are looking for projects or commitments that you believe are inhibiting your ability to effectively perform the red-zone activities in your life. These commitments may be very good things that you took on with the best of intentions and sincere optimism but that are now beginning to become more obligation than opportunity. They may also be brand-new ideas or opportunities that you feel a strong urge to act on but that are ill timed because of the lack of hours or resources to devote to them.

Some questions to ask when evaluating potentially prune-able activities are:

- Is this having a negative impact on my red-zone efforts or my overall ability to stay energized in my life and work?
- Has this become more obligation than opportunity? Have I lost my passion for and interest in this?
- Could this be deferred until later and have a greater effect?
- Am I unhappy with my current results?
- Do I have a nagging sense that I need to go in a new direction with this project?

If the answer is yes to any of these questions, then you may want to consider eliminating the project from your plate. As you do, you will likely find that the increased space in your life yields new insights and ideas for your more pressing projects.

Another thing to consider is that saying no doesn't mean forever. You're just trying to make sure that the places where you're choosing to expend your energy are appropriate for the priorities of the season. It's likely that something you say no to today will become one of your top priorities next month. You need to give yourself permission regarding what you're choosing *not* to work on as well as what you *are* choosing to work on. David Allen teaches a principle in his book *Getting Things Done* called the "Someday/Maybe" list that is an effective repository for projects that you want to begin at some point but not now. Keeping a list of "someday I will . . ." kinds of projects allows you to put things off without feeling like you are abandoning them forever.

Pruning Yields New Opportunities

One woman I worked with, a video editor named Susan, is an avid gardener. In a conversation about the principle of pruning, she observed that whenever she pruned back a single branch in her garden, two new growths would emerge. Pruning activities in our life often seems to work the same way. Don't be surprised if your willingness to endure a little temporary discomfort by cutting away good but ill-timed projects and opportunities yields an abundant harvest of new ideas and exciting prospects.

Be wise about the commitments you make and the way in which you manage your energy. It could be the single greatest determining factor in whether you are the superstar who burns out on the altar of short-term productivity or the one who thrives for a lifetime.

It's difficult to separate good energy management from the proper management of time, stimuli, focus, and relationships. Each of these areas of rhythm affects each of the others. Don't be surprised, for instance, if your newly implemented practices around energy begin to give you a greater sense of enthusiasm to the relationships in your life.

Similarly, without a good strategy for managing the energy in your life, there will be little you can do to maintain your effectiveness over the long term. The practices we've discussed in this chapter are a good starting point for preventing overload and staying creatively focused, but I've included a list of other resources at AccidentalCreative.com/book if you'd like further insights into the subject.

STIMULI:
WHAT GOES IN
MUST COME OUT

7.

We are swimming in a sea of information. Every day, we are bombarded by thousands of inputs, from advertising jingles to plot twists on our favorite TV shows. Some of this information is received in the context of our daily work, and much of it is a result of our reading or viewing habits and the time we spend surfing the web or rifling through magazines.

What we don't often consider is how these messages affect our capacity to do our best creative work. It goes without saying that what we put into our heads will necessarily influence what and how well we create.

In a famed illustration of how environmental stimuli subconsciously affect our mental processes, British "psychological illusionist" Derren Brown invited two members of an ad agency to pitch concepts for a chain of taxidermy stores he was proposing to build. The ad execs, with no prior knowledge of why they were being summoned, were taken on a long taxi ride, then escorted into an office building where they were given instructions and told they had just thirty minutes to develop a poster for the chain, including store name, a tagline, and visuals. Brown also placed a sealed envelope containing his own concepts on a table, to be opened later.

After thirty minutes elapsed, Brown reappeared in the room to check on their work. The execs pitched a concept they called "Animal Heaven," featuring an illustration of a bear playing a lyre and the tagline "the best place for dead animals." After their pitch, Brown asked one of the execs to open the envelope he'd placed in the room at the very beginning. To their surprise, the envelope contained a nearly identical treatment of the poster, including a very similar bear holding a lyre and a similar tagline.

Brown went on to show viewers that the taxi ride to the office building had strategically featured several items designed to draw the attention of the ad execs. These items, such as a conspicuously placed lyre, a poster with the phrase "The Best Place for Dead Animals," and a trip past the London Zoo, had made subconscious impressions that were quick to reemerge as they scrambled to generate concepts.

With the ever-increasing deluge of information we all face, the task for each of us is to discern which inputs are relevant to our work and which are simply noise. We face tremendous pressure to keep up and the vast majority of creatives I work with say they are constantly on the verge of information overload.

But it's not just the sheer amount of information that's the problem; if it were that simple, we could just shut it off. The real challenge is that some of this onslaught of information is necessary for us to perform our jobs, whether it's e-mail, blogs, trend reports, or industry news. We must somehow engage with the information that enters our daily lives, process it, and turn it into something meaningful.

Bryn Mooth, editor of the design magazine *HOW,* told me in an interview that she compares this struggle to working with a food processor.

"A food processor has a small intake, and a huge work bowl," she says. "All of the food has to get through the processor, but there's only so much capacity at any given time. This is similar to how we must deal with the overload of new information we experience every day. We simply don't have the capacity to process all of the information in a timely way with our limited mental resources." She continued that she frequently advises creatives to closely monitor the quality of what they choose to absorb because it is so closely tied to their creative process.

While our minds are unparalleled in their capacity to experience and assimilate information, they also have a limited bandwidth for doing so. As a matter of survival, they tend to weed out information that is deemed irrelevant to our immediate needs. However, our minds are also capable of taking random bits of input and forging brilliant connections that are not apparent on the surface. This is essentially how the creative process works—it's the connection of multiple preexisting patterns into new solutions. One pathway to creating more effectively and consistently is to be strategic about our inputs.

> **While our minds are unparalleled in their capacity to experience and assimilate information, they also have a limited bandwidth for doing so.**

YOUR DIET OF STIMULI

I call the information and experiences we absorb "stimuli" because these are the raw materials that stimulate thought. Each creative idea is the combination of previously existing ideas, or bits of stimuli, into something new. The stimuli we experience can stretch us to think differently, to open our eyes to new ways of seeing the world. But many creatives don't give much thought to what they allow into their minds. E-mails, reports, web videos, TV, magazines, and more flood through their life with no one

STIMULI

keeping watch of the gate. Over time this can result in an overall lack of focus or a general numbness to potential inspiration. Discerning what is useful and what isn't in a world without filters on our stimuli becomes a difficult task. After all, a drowning man isn't thinking about what he wants for dinner, he just wants a life preserver! In the same way, when we lack structure around the types of stimuli we experience, we lack the space and focus we need to apply our experiences to the work we're engaged in.

There is an old saying about health and nutrition, that "you are what you eat." This means that the kinds of food you put into your body will ultimately affect your physical being and your mobility and interaction with the world. If you regularly consume junk food rather than healthy, nutritious food, your health will eventually fail. If, however, you ensure that the staples of your diet are healthy and nutritious, you can occasionally snack on junk food with little concern. It's all about choice and following healthy principles with regard to diet.

This same principle applies to cultivating a healthy diet of stimuli in your life. Because so much of the information you must process in a given day is determined by the nature of your work, you need to be purposeful about including self-directed, thought-provoking, and capacity-increasing stimuli into your life on a consistent basis. Whether it's in the form of print media, movies, web videos, conversations, advertisements, or anything else that is delivering a message you must process and assimilate, the stimuli you take in over the course of your day informs the quality of the insights you generate. Just like good food increases your capacity to be active and healthy, the higher the quality of your stimuli, the better you are setting yourself up for high-level breakthroughs.

Larry Kelley, chief planning officer at Houston-based ad agency FKM, and author of *Advertising Account Planning*, says that he has used our methods for cultivating better stimuli to help FKM's team generate more effective ideas for their clients.

"Why would you go to the museum of art to learn more about

a steak restaurant? Because it led to a breakthrough idea for turning a place you eat a steak into a place where you experience the finer things in the world. When we got stuck on the project we looked for different, but relevant stimuli that might give us a new perspective. In this case, rather than focus our attention on the restaurant category advertising, most of which is all the same, we brought in stimuli that offered a different viewpoint. I've learned from Accidental Creative that you are what you take in, so as a team we always try to take in the best."

In this case, Larry and his team understood that the solution to their creative problems was unlikely to come from staring harder at the problem, but would instead be found by immersing themselves in higher-quality stimuli. What are some characteristics that mark higher quality stimuli?

It's challenging. We want stimuli that will help us grow in our capacity to comprehend complex things. Pop culture is helpful for keeping up with trends (and for entertainment, of course), but we also need to commune with great minds and experience mind-stretching concepts and ideas that challenge our existing view of the world. This helps us break through mental ruts and consider new options that were previously obscured by our assumptions. While there's nothing wrong with catching a sitcom or two throughout your week, you may also want to structure time into your life to watch documentaries on stimulating subjects.

It's relevant. This doesn't mean that we should be looking only for stimuli that offer specific solutions to the creative problems we are facing, but it does mean that when we are working on highly intense projects, we should somewhat limit our stimuli to materials that will help our minds focus more effectively on those problems. Are there leaders in your industry who have published papers or articles that may help you think in new ways about your work? Are there trend reports that may help you think through where your business is headed next? A good rule of thumb is that every single day should include some kind of stimuli that is directed at your personal growth (working through a book, studying a skill or technique, et cetera) and some kind of stimuli that you've sought out for purposes of advancing your work (an industry trend report, a research study, a trade magazine).

It's diverse. While carrots are healthy for me, if I eat nothing but carrots for a few months I will probably find my body in serious disrepair. Similarly, we must diversify our diet of stimuli by exploring divergent topics of interest, by varying forms of media, and by ingesting the opinions of others we may be inclined to disagree with. This diversification will expand our capacity to process information, help us form new and interesting thought patterns, and stimulate different parts of our brain than would be triggered if we were to continue in the same stimulus rut.

Another thing to consider with regard to diversity is that often our next great breakthrough is more likely to come from outside our industry or area of expertise than from within it. When we diversify our base of stimuli, however, it forces us to approach problems from a new perspective. Ben Nicholson, creative director at the video production house Lightborne, likes to look in nonintuitive places for inspiration in his work. He once shared short stories and essays with his team as inspiration for new projects, something pretty far outside the realm of video work. But this diversity of stimuli prevents the team from falling into ruts or unknowingly imitating industry trends.

As you consider the diet of stimuli in your life, these three factors should play a role in the decision.

STAYING AHEAD OF THE PRESSURE

Another key benefit of being purposeful about the stimuli in your life is that you can direct your mind to begin working on problems before your need for ideas becomes urgent. For example, if there is a big project on the horizon that requires you to have an understanding of a specific topic, then it is a good idea to get a head start on the project by choosing stimuli that will lay the foundation for that understanding. You may want to do a little research to find the highest-rated or most recommended book on a particular subject. You may want to start reading a blog or two that covers emerging trends in this area and their cultural effects.

Our minds require time to do their best work, and the more of a head start and the healthier a perspective we can give them, the more likely it is that we will uncover novel and relevant patterns. Not only that, but the more grounded we are in the subject matter, the easier it is for us to discern relevant versus irrelevant data. It's almost as if we gain a sixth sense about problem solving once we are deeply immersed in relevant stimuli.

There are three practices in the remainder of this chapter that I've found tremendously helpful for myself and for my clients in processing and assimilating information in a way that will be useful in the creative process. The practices, which are designed to instill rhythm and purpose into the stimuli we absorb, can be divided into three categories: cultivate, process, and experience.

CULTIVATE: THE STUDY PLAN

Maintaining a study plan will help you cultivate the kinds of stimuli you allow into your life and ensure that you are putting the most important pieces in place first. I have used one for years, and it has made a tremendous difference in my exposure to great thinkers, my understanding of key issues at work, and my ability to process new and complex thoughts. I consult and revise it regularly—typically in my monthly checkpoints (more on these later)—as a way to make sure that I'm continuing to challenge myself with the things I choose to allow in my head.

Can you list the last three books you read? How about the last three magazines you perused? The last three movies you saw? How about the last ten web pages you visited? If you're like many people, you'll probably need to think a minute to answer these questions, if you even can. Because we often approach the stimuli in our life randomly and without any kind of formal structure, there are few intuitive connecting points between them, and, as a result, we draw few if any lasting insights from having experienced them. Anything we might have gained is forgotten as quickly as we turn our attention to something new.

> **"I must study politics and war that my sons may have liberty to study mathematics and philosophy."**
>
> **—John Adams**

Again, our minds are excellent at receiving new information, forging new patterns out of it, and then assimilating those patterns. But the more random the information you absorb, the more effort is required to process it and utilize it in your creative work. Variety is certainly helpful in forcing you to look outside your normal handful of solutions to the creative problems you face, but it can also lead you down irrelevant rabbit trails or cause you to feel overwhelmed. If you are more purposeful in how you structure the stimuli you experience, however, you can gently nudge your mind in a direction where creative insights are more likely to occur.

The practice of deliberate study plays an important role in the development of your capacity to think and to process new information. When you assemble a study plan, you cultivate a queue of stimuli designed to grow your creative capacity. Your ability to synthesize new ideas is largely influenced by your depth and breadth of knowledge in diverse domains of expertise. As you study you develop networks of understanding that connect various bits of data in your daily life into meaningful patterns. The more you strengthen these networks of understanding through study, the larger they grow. Similarly, as you diversify your areas of study, you are able to make connections between various domains of knowledge. The net benefit of this greater understanding of the world is that you are capable of generating more novel and appropriate creative insights. You can more easily derive metaphors and see the similarities or connecting points between problems you're facing. As this understanding grows stronger, your platform for creative expression grows proportionately.

As Benjamin and Rosamund Zander write in *The Art of Possibility*, "The frames our minds create define—and confine—what we perceive to be possible. Every problem, every dilemma, every dead-end we face in life, only appears unsolvable inside a particular frame or point of view. Enlarge the box, or create another frame around the data, and problems vanish, while new opportunities appear." Purposefully structuring stimuli in your life through the practice of study enlarges your framework for understanding the world and allows you to synthesize more appropriate solutions to your creative problems.

Structuring Your Study Plan

Structure your study plan in quarterly increments. This will give you enough of a horizon to ensure that you are getting ahead of your work without planning so far ahead that it becomes impossible to know which stimuli will provide the most appropriate foundation for your upcoming work. There are three criteria you want to apply when determining what should make the cut for your study plan:

Where are you lacking information that you will need over the next three months? What will help you engage with your work more effectively? Are there any gaps of experience or knowledge that could become blind spots and prevent you from doing your best work?

Again, with time on your side, you can be more purposeful about closing those knowledge gaps, and you can be more selective about how you do it. Maybe you need to read a book, peruse some old magazine articles, or line up a few conversations with experts in order to gain the insights you need. The main thing is that you are being purposeful in moving your mind in a specific direction. This "I need information for work" category should take up about a quarter of your study time.

What are you curious about right now? Your study plan is not just a method for getting more done at work; it's also a method for growing yourself intellectually, emotionally, and spiritually. Take note of where your curiosity leads you in various areas of your life and give yourself permission to explore those curiosities. So often the overwhelming flood of information we're required to process on a daily basis squeezes out any time we might have for pursuing personal interests. By structuring these areas of curiosity into your study plan, you ensure that you're allotting time and attention for cultivating your passions and growing your capacity to explore the deeper questions you have about the world around you.

Your personal curiosities can range from broad subject matter (mathematics, physics, ancient Rome, the Revolutionary War) to specific skills you'd like to learn (cooking, gardening, woodworking). Pursue these subjects because you're personally passionate about them, not out of obligation. These are your guilty pleasures, although there's nothing to feel guilty about. In fact, this category should make up about half of your study plan.

What would be good for you? This part of your study plan is the equivalent of eating your mental vegetables. Some items need to be a part of your study plan because they stretch your mind, cause you to grow in new ways, or help expand your worldview. When considering this category, think about areas where you may be deficient in some way, where you have an educational blind spot, where you need to gain more information that could be useful down the road. This category should make up the final quarter of your study plan.

In his book *The Contrarian's Guide to Leadership*, author and USC president Stephen Sample suggests that we spend the majority of our study time focusing on what he calls the "supertexts." These are the works that have stood the test of time—Sample uses the examples of Machiavelli's *The Prince*, various religious texts, and Plato's *Republic*—in other words, texts proven by longevity to speak to the deeper human condition. Sample's point is that much of the content that is produced today is simply derivative of these supertexts, and not nearly as helpful in forming our understanding of how the world works or forging useful patterns of knowledge. Rather than reading the derivatives, Sample believes that we'd be better served to go directly to the sources. He also includes among the supertexts great literary works, plays, spiritual texts, and fiction that have lasted for decades or centuries. I've adopted Sample's recommendation and have found that reading great works not only stretches my creative expression but also helps me identify patterns in human behavior that haven't changed much over time. In many ways, it's like communing with the great minds of history and allowing them to illuminate your understanding of how the world works. This improved understanding increases your platform for expression and creative problem solving.

Remember that this study plan is not intended to be the sum total of all the stimuli you absorb in your life. It's simply meant to provide a supporting infrastructure for your thought life and to ensure that there is some purpose and intentionality behind the kinds of stimuli that inform your creative process. The study plan, and your study time, will help you maintain stability and rhythm. Anything else you choose to absorb is fine as long as you're building in the most critical stuff first. You can feel less guilty about mindlessly surfing the web or watching reality TV if you know that you have time and energy set aside to explore more purposeful, insight-yielding stimuli.

Once you have determined the items that will be a part of your study plan, you may want to keep a Stimulus Queue. This is a place where you keep a list of items you plan to read, experience, or study. The most effective practice is to establish regular times for study in your schedule, then to work through your queue in sequential order during those times. Again, this will ensure that you are getting to the things that matter and are not simply drifting to whatever happens to capture your attention at any given moment. My study time has fluctuated depending on the season, but I've typically maintained one at 5:30 a.m. each weekday, and it lasts for about an hour. Other creatives I've worked with prefer to study at night because they find it a good release from the pressures of the day. Other creatives I've coached prefer to do it over their lunch break. Regardless of when, the critical principle is that your study time is consistent and nonnegotiable.

During this time I work sequentially through the items in my Stimulus Queue, whether it means reading a certain number of pages from a book, reading a few magazine articles, listening to podcasts, or experiencing something else entirely. While I also read at various times throughout the day, and I am always listening to audio books in my car or on walks. This structured study time ensures that my personal mental development and the cultivation of my curiosity never succumbs to the busyness of the work day. Because of scheduling issues, others may need to break up their study time into increments, perhaps a half hour in the morning for personal growth and work-related study, and a half hour at night for personal study. (For a complete list of recommended tools you can use to keep your Stimulus Queue in order, visit AccidentalCreative.com/book.)

What will you study? How will you structure purposeful development into your life? By doing so you are cultivating the soil and planting the seeds for future creative insights.

CONVERTING INFORMATION TO WISDOM TO CREATIVE INSIGHT

There is a significant difference between information and wisdom. But in a culture that is obsessed with sound bites and snack-sized media, wisdom is increasingly taking a backseat to perpetual stimulation. The danger in this is that we stop thinking "what's best?" and instead worry only about "what's next?"

In *Birth of the Chaordic Age*, VISA International founder Dee Hock shares some thoughts on how raw information is transformed by our minds into something more useful. Hock argues that noise becomes data when it is grouped into a pattern, when you can identify a noticeable and memorable connection between bits of noise. He continues to show the progression of data to wisdom as it becomes increasingly structured and useful in our day-to-day decisions.

If you want to turn the noise in your environment into something useful, you must develop systems for filtering stimuli and discerning which of it is most relevant to your work. But then you must go a step further and actually learn to utilize this stimuli in your creative process in a meaningful way. The resulting benefit of a purposeful approach to stimuli is the ability to think more systemically and cultivate a deeper understanding of the world at large. In other words, you develop wisdom. This begins with becoming more observant and capturing insights in the moment.

PROCESS: NOTATION

The goal of study is not simply to absorb a lot of new information. You want to process and assimilate it, then apply it to your life and work. If you don't cultivate insights from what you take in, then the value of stimuli in your life decreases dramatically. Taking good notes on your observations, insights, and experiences with a reliable thought-capture system prevents them from disappearing into the ether.

> **"He listens well who takes notes."**
>
> **—Dante Alighieri**

In the moment, we always think we'll remember our best ideas later, but many of us have learned the hard way that even the most profound insights can be fleeting. How many times has a solution to a problem suddenly popped into your head and seemed so obvious that you thought there was no way you could forget it, and then you almost immediately did? This has happened to me too many times to count. This fleeting thought was often something critical to my work. After getting burned this way a few too many times, I made a practice of taking regular notes throughout my day and of carrying a small notebook or index card with me as a way to record insights and prompts that may be useful later.

We all know that note taking is important, but usually our notes are limited to facts, to-dos, meeting outlines, and so on. While these kinds of notes are certainly useful, they're often shuffled into the back of a notebook or file folder and never looked at again. They're more notes of record than useful fodder for our creative process.

Observations and insights, on the other hand, often go unrecorded. These include anything from questions that arise in the course of a meeting to intuitions we have that we don't deem noteworthy because they aren't something we think we'll be required to know later. This is unfortunate, because these little insights could be seeds of brilliance. You need to cultivate an attitude of active listening, which includes actively listening to your own thoughts and responses in the moment to whatever you're experiencing.

Many great and creative minds of history have made a practice of voracious note taking as a way of sorting their thoughts and processing their experiences. In his acclaimed biography of John Adams, David McCullough writes of Adams's habit of making notes in the margins of his books. "At times the marginal observations nearly equaled what was printed on the page," he explains, "as in Mary Wollstonecraft's *French Revolution*, which Adams read at least twice and with delight, since he disagreed with nearly everything she said. To her claim that government must be simple, for example, he answered, 'The clock would be simple if you destroyed all the wheels . . . but it would not tell the time of day.'"

Adams was not taking notes the way that many of us have been taught, by making lists or mindlessly underlining key passages. Rather, he was recording his own thoughts and reactions to the claims of the author. He treated books as a conversation rather than a monologue. Unlike Adams, many of us stop listening to our own thoughts and reactions when we're engaging with something external. We fail to realize that our instinctual reactions, if we learn to pay attention to them, can be indicators of something brilliant lurking just beneath the surface.

Staying alert and paying attention to how you're reacting to an experience, a book, or a conversation also forces you to stay out of ruts that could prevent creative insights. Rather than mindlessly moving through your day, you can actively engage by learning to reflectively ask questions and record your responses. Here are some questions that can serve as a starting point for making your notes more effective:

Are there any patterns in what you're experiencing (or reading) that are similar to something else you're working on? Often the solutions to

STIMULI

your problems will come in the form of analogy or metaphor. If you look for similarities between your day-to-day experiences and the problems you're working on, you may find unexpected connections. Even works of fiction, movies you watch, or conversations you have may contain patterns that can be helpful in solving your creative problems. You just need to be mindful to watch for them and take good notes when you notice them.

What do you find surprising about what you're experiencing? Surprise can be an indicator of an entrenched belief that needs to be challenged. You should pay attention to surprises throughout your day because they may mark pathways to insight that are as of yet unexplored. Surprise reactions can also illuminate areas of curiosity for potential further study.

What do you like about what you're experiencing and why? Exploring your personal preferences can be a great way to understand your habits or creative tendencies. You should aspire to stay actively aware of your preferences.

What do you dislike about what you're experiencing? Sometimes your reaction against something will yield helpful insights, especially if it reveals assumptions you're holding on to about the way things "have to be."

"The test of a first-rate intelligence is the ability to hold two opposing ideas in mind at the same time and still retain the ability to function," F. Scott Fitzgerald once wrote. "One should, for example, be able to see that things are hopeless yet be determined to make them otherwise." Your willingness to process your opposition to something—rather than simply ignoring it when it disagrees with your current view of the world—increases your capacity to synthesize ideas out of seemingly unrelated stimuli. You should note these thoughts in the moment rather than overlooking them.

In addition to making good observations and regularly recording them, you should also make a practice of regularly reviewing your notes to see if there are any potentially applicable insights. Many creatives I've worked with take copious notes, but they're practically useless because they're always moving on to the next urgent matter, and thus they never bother to review them. One manager I encountered had pages and pages of detailed notes on every meeting she'd attended in the past month, one-on-one meetings with her direct reports, and potential upcoming projects. She never reviewed them, however, because they weren't really useful. They consisted of only facts and memorandums but nothing truly useful in her work, such as patterns she was noticing or creative ideas that emerged in the conversation. I explained that her notes would be significantly more helpful if she would record what's truly useful, then make the time in her life to reflect on them and look for applications to her work, which she vowed to try.

Author Keith Ferrazzi told me in an interview that he spends an average of an hour each day thinking about and processing information that he's taken in the previous day. He believes that the processing of information is as critical as the information he takes in. While not all of us can spend that much time purely in processing mode, the principle certainly holds true that we are overlooking the real benefit of our experiences if we never stop to reflect on them. Take the time each day to review your notes and observations from the previous day.

Tools of the Trade

I once oversaw an event featuring John Pepper, chairman of the Walt Disney Company and former CEO of Procter & Gamble. After the event, as we were standing in a reception area for a meet-and-greet, I noticed that Mr. Pepper would occasionally reach into his jacket pocket, pull out an index card, and jot a note on it. This happened several times over the course of a few minutes. When someone in the reception line said something in conversation that sparked a thought, or would require later follow-up, he would covertly pull out his index card and write a few words.

This experience prompted me to adopt a practice that I've since used to great effect, which is to keep a small stack of index cards with me at all times for use in taking notes and recording observations. I place a fresh index card in every book I'm reading, or start a new one for every meeting I have. I keep the used index cards in my bag or in my notebook for review the next morning. When I review them I look for action steps, potentially useful thoughts, or just ideas I want to act on. This kind of nonlinear, nonchronological note taking allows me to be liberal in capturing insights and tidbits in the moment, and then to review them at my leisure.

When I pick up a book, I will quickly review the index card with my notes from the previous session so that I know what I was thinking when I left off. If I am going into a meeting, I will review my notes from the previous meeting to ensure that I understand what the important issues are. I try to record any thought that comes to mind, even if it seems like a non sequitur at the moment. I often discover later that the thought was more relevant than I realized because my mind was at work on something interesting behind the scenes. If I hadn't developed the practice of notation, it would have been lost forever.

Using a Notebook for Effective Note Taking

If you prefer to use a notebook for your note taking, I'd recommend that you begin by numbering each of the pages of your notebook. This will serve as a reference for indexing and referencing ideas.

Next, create two index pages in the front of your notebook. At the top of the first index write "Ideas," and at the top of the second write "Stimuli." Whenever you have an insight or idea that you think may be useful at some point in the future, record the headline of the idea in the index in the front of your notebook along with its corresponding page number. These ideas could be small insights that you think could later turn into big ones, or even just observations you make that you think could be useful later. For example, if you had an idea to create a web-based community for rugby players to help them find matches in their area, and you explored the idea on pages 77–78 of your notebook, you would proceed to the index and record "pp. 77–78 / Create a Web community for rugby players." Later, as you are looking for ideas for projects or simply wanting to refresh your memory of past ideas, you can quickly review the index for something potentially useful. This is also a great way to be able to search past notebooks without having to thumb through every page looking for a single idea.

Additionally, whenever you come across stimuli that you think would make good candidates for your Stimulus Queue, record them in the index in the front of your notebook. Write the names of books and their authors, movie trailers that appeal to you, or magazine articles that you notice in the doctor's office and want to revisit later. If you take notes from a conversation and someone mentions a useful resource, you can also record the page number of the notes from your conversation in the index so that you have context for why you thought a particular piece of stimulus would be interesting.

Finally, make a habit of regularly reviewing your idea and stimuli indexes. When you're stuck on a project, glance back over them to see if there are any useful ideas. I recommend that you develop the habit at the beginning of each day of reviewing the ideas in your index. One of your ideas may suddenly be relevant to the work you're doing that day or help you identify new ways of thinking about your creative problems.

Digital Versus Electronic Note Taking

As an early adopter and tech junkie, I completely empathize if you prefer to take your notes digitally. I've used a number of methods for digital note taking, and I still use a combination of my phone and my computer to capture and sync notes in many circumstances. But there are significant disadvantages to going completely digital.

First, unless you remember to review your notes on a regular basis, they can easily disappear, tucked into some virtual folder where you will never think to look for them again. (With paper notes, there is always a physical reminder sitting on your desk.) Also, while digital notes are infinitely more searchable and sortable, they are also more limiting when it comes to sketching out an idea or a quick chart. Even with some of the new tablet devices, to quickly and effectively capture thoughts when you're pushing pixels instead of ink can be difficult and awkward.

Regardless of the method you choose, though, it's critical not to neglect the practice of note taking. As a starting place, simply carry an index card, a small notebook, or your digital note-taking device everywhere, and whenever you have an interesting thought, even if it seems completely random and unrelated to anything you're working on, record it. Over time you will begin to see patterns in your thoughts and preferences, and will likely gain at least a few ideas each week that otherwise would have been overlooked.

> Regularly reviewing your notes is critical to staying alert to potential ideas.

Additionally, it's critical that you take time regularly to process your notes so that you are able to identify patterns and insights. Remember: the goal of taking notes is to extract potentially useful connections and ideas. Make time each day to review your notes from the previous day and regularly review them for insights that could be useful in your present work. Here's a morning note-review routine that you may want to implement:

- Clear ten minutes at the very beginning of your workday. If necessary, plan to arrive ten minutes earlier, or if taking a train or bus, use your commute time. (Please do not do this while driving to work!)
- If you keep notes in multiple places, collect any index cards or meeting notes from the previous day, and your notebook. If you are taking notes electronically, do a filter so that you can view only notes created the previous day.
- Review the index cards and meeting notes for insights or ideas that are especially useful. You may want to transfer these to your notebook and record them in your index. Similarly, if there are potentially useful stimuli in your notes, you will want to record these in your stimulus index.
- Review your notes from any stimuli you experienced/ read/watched yesterday.
- Scan through your list of ideas for anything that may be useful in the work you will be doing today.
- If you have any new ideas while reviewing your notes, go ahead and record them in your notebook and in the index.

Again, without regular review, the practice of note taking is fairly useless. It's not about recording what's happened; it's about how what's happened has affected or inspired you. By reviewing them regularly you increase the likelihood that they will be useful to you and that you won't forget critical insights when things get hectic.

EXPERIENCE: EXPLORING YOUR WORLD

With all this emphasis on study and reflection, you don't want to neglect actual experiences. You absorb much of your understanding of the world through sensory interaction and experiment,

STIMULI

and to ignore this would be to cut yourself off from the most significant source of inspiration. You need to regularly seek experiences that will enlighten you, help you see the world in new ways, and open you to new ways of thinking.

Much has been written regarding the importance of play to our growth and development. Play is the primary way children learn, and recent research has shown that play can contribute significantly to the learning of adults as well. Play helps us maintain emotional stability, too, which can be important to our overall energy level and capacity for good work.

In his recent book *Play*, author Stuart Brown argues that "play is the stick that stirs the drink. It is the basis of all art, games, books, sports, movies, fashion, fun, and wonder—in short, the basis of what we think of as civilization. Play is the vital essence of life. It is what makes life lively." As we grow older, Brown believes, we tend to weed out any activity that isn't immediately productive or profitable. We eliminate play because it's not expedient to our immediate needs. In doing so, we turn our back on a primary tool for creative inspiration and growth.

Many of us are caught in the same routines and patterns day after day and week after week. We rarely venture outside these routines because they have proven effective for us. While it's admirable to be disciplined and focused, we don't want to leave great creative insights on the table simply because we'd rather stay in our comfort zone. We must deliberately build new, different, and challenging experiences into our lives. This means setting aside time to put ourselves in stimulating and even purposefully uncomfortable situations so that our minds are forced to see the world in new ways. Here are just a few suggestions for how to do this:

Take a walk around a local park or make a trip to a local museum. What catches your attention? Is there anything that seems strange to you or piques your curiosity? What have you not noticed before? Be purposeful and mindful. Turn off your phone. Naturally, you will take your notebook with you. Record any thoughts or insights that pop into mind. Don't be afraid to record thoughts that don't relate to your work. It's possible that insights formed here may develop into something very valuable down the road. If you can't get to a park or museum, just take thirty minutes over lunch, leave your phone on your desk, and go for a quick walk around the block.

More than once I've told certain members of my team to get out of the office. Leave, and don't come back—until you're refreshed. While this seems unproductive on the surface, we've often seen breakthroughs for key projects come as a direct result. Team members will come back with excited looks in their eyes and say, "I was walking around a bookstore and saw . . ." or "I was in the park and I thought . . ." The value that results from these small breaks is immeasurable, whereas having a team sitting around pushing pixels in the attempt to look productive is actually significantly less productive.

Serve others. When we are forced to think less about ourselves and are instead required to think about the needs of others, something is unlocked inside us. Because creative work can be very consuming, we can get lost in an endless pursuit of our personal needs. Making a break from thinking about ourselves and our problems for a while often frees up insight that is lurking just beneath the surface. Our act of service doesn't have to be anything significant or earth changing. You can get involved in youth mentorship, coach a kids sports team, or serve at a local soup kitchen. The main thing is that you stop worrying about yourself for a while and instead focus on serving others. Not only do you benefit creatively from this, but you also get to change the world in small but significant ways.

Attend an uncomfortable event. Make plans to attend a lecture by someone who holds a differing point of view. Visit a religious service that is outside of your own tradition or comfort zone. If you are an introvert, go to a dance club or a party. If you are an extrovert, spend some extended time on your own. A good gauge for this is to ask yourself, "What makes me uncomfortable just thinking about doing it?" The goal is to stretch yourself, to resist the temptation to gravitate toward comfort. In so many ways, comfort is the enemy of creativity. When we default to comfort out of fear of the unknown, we often ignore the paths that may change our life. Taking small steps to put ourselves in uncomfortable situations is one way of interrupting the comfort-seeking pattern.

> **Making a break from thinking about ourselves and our problems for a while often frees up insight that is lurking just beneath the surface.**

The purpose of structuring purposeful experiences into our life is to grow the reservoir from which we draw insights. Much has been written on this subject over time, but common sense is not common practice. Some of the very things that are most helpful to our creative process seem like common sense, but we must not make the tragic mistake of dismissing them because of that.

Question: What experience will you structure into your life this week in order to stretch your thinking and challenge your perspective?

With ever-expanding access to entertainment and news, it can be tempting to snack on information all day indiscriminately, but if you want to be sharp and do your best work, you must become more purposeful about what you are putting into your mind. Purposefully structuring the stimuli in your life provides the foundation for your work and increases the chances you will experience creative breakthroughs.

Don't feel the need, however, to be overly strict about this. Just like with our food diet, it's all right to eat junk from time to time. There's nothing wrong with surfing the web or reading pop culture magazines for pleasure. In fact, many great ideas will come from these activities, but it's important not to make the junk a staple of your diet. The really effective stimuli are the ones that shape your thinking, increase your knowledge base, and stretch your understanding of the world. You need to be purposeful about building these kinds of healthy, capacity-increasing stimuli into your life.

HOURS: THEY'RE THE CURRENCY OF PRODUCTIVITY

8.

Since the invention of the clock, people have been obsessed with time. Walk through any bookstore and you'll find advice—on saving it, organizing it, squeezing more out of it—filling shelf after shelf of self-help literature. There are countless time-management philosophies and systems available, and new gurus appear on the scene practically every day promising to help us put some order into our hectic life. Websites that share "life hacks" and promise to make us more productive get millions of visits per year. Much of this advice is predicated on the assumption that time is a finite resource and that we must maximize every spare moment of productive capacity. Many of us are looking for a system or a trick to help us do just that.

There are so many demands on your time, it's easy to feel no control over where your time is spent. We all feel the persistent ticking of the clock in the back of our minds. Seconds are slipping away and with every moment we're getting closer to our deadlines. After all, isn't there something else you should probably be doing right now instead of reading this? Is this really the best way to spend your time? Isn't there something more productive that you could be doing? Shouldn't you check your e-mail, make a quick call, or review your task list?

> **"We say we waste time, but that is impossible. We waste ourselves."**
>
> **—Alice Bloch**

To be honest, it took every ounce of resistance in me not to check my e-mail in the middle of writing that sentence. Why do we feel a constant pull toward things like e-mail and task lists? Sure, it feels good when we can check something off our list or send a response to an e-mail that's been staring us down for a few hours, but what we often neglect in our pursuit of productivity nirvana is that some of the tasks we gravitate to are interfering with more important, capacity-building work. We unwittingly become slaves to the task.

Driving this insecurity is the belief that time is the currency of productivity. At the end of the day, if we've spent it in the right place, we win. If we've spent it in the wrong place, we lose. Whenever we fail to do what's needed, we accumulate a debt that will have to be repaid at some point. After all, our work isn't going away, and someone has to do it. At the same time, we often obsess unnecessarily about our time because we grow paranoid that we're constantly losing ground or that we're somehow going to fall behind and never be able to dig out of work debt. For many creatives, this mind-set results from the fact that they are constantly reacting to the workload rather than giving themselves the space needed to get ahead of it.

I think a lot of us feel this way, whether we realize it or not. This insecurity about time is one of the main things that causes us, even unknowingly, to cram work into every available crevice in our life. We are perpetually thinking, moving pieces around in our head, and problem solving. We feel the pressure to produce, and we know that we need to use our time wisely to do so. But as mentioned earlier in the book, this always-on mind-set unknowingly causes us to forfeit our best work.

Of the five elements of rhythm discussed in this book, time is the most significant pressure point for many creatives. It's where we feel the biggest crunch, because it's the most concrete resource that we need to allocate toward our work each day. It's also the one element that provides the foundation for our practices in each of the other areas. As a result, developing a healthy mind-set toward your time is critical, and not just in terms of how you crank through tasks or how efficiently you conduct meetings. While these things have their place, you need to be just as mindful of what's not present in your life and how this is affecting your creative capacity as well. Though it's counterintuitive, the solution to feeling overwhelmed or crunched for time is often not to remove something from your life, but to add something that raises your level of effectiveness in those activities you're already doing.

ALL MINUTES ARE NOT CREATED EQUAL

There is much advice on how to organize your time to conquer your tasks, but it is mostly predicated on the assumption that your goal is simply to get *through* the work, with little regard to the quality of that work. But this is simply not the case. As a creative, you are held to account for the quality of your work, not just the quantity.

Each project you take on makes demands of your time. You are forced to make priority calls about where you're going to spend your hours, and because of the pressure of scarcity, you probably frequently feel like you have one chance to get it right.

What we often overlook is that one hour effectively spent can produce better results than five hours spent on a lot of frenetic activity. Breakthroughs can happen in a brief moment, but these kinds of sudden breakthroughs result from a lifestyle of structuring your time according to an effectiveness mind-set rather than an efficiency one.

> **"Lost time is never found again."**
>
> **—Benjamin Franklin**

Warning: In the rest of this chapter I will be asking you to commit time to specific practices that will make you more effective. You will be tempted to think, *There's no way I could do this stuff—I don't have the time.* I'd like to challenge you to focus on how you can incorporate these disciplines rather than on all the reasons you can't.

THE PORTFOLIO AND THE SLOT MACHINE

As creatives, our value to the organization is determined by what we create, not for how much time we spend creating it. We have only so much idea generation time to go around, so we need to get the most out of what we have. It's counterintuitive, but if we want to increase our productive output, we need to let go of our stranglehold on time. We must learn to spend our time effectively rather than obsessing about efficiency. To spend our time effectively means that we are willing to view our time as a portfolio of investments, not as a slot machine.

We put our money in a slot machine hoping that the next pull of the lever will pay off. The more coins we gamble, the closer we think we're getting to a jackpot, but the odds of the game remain the same. No matter how many pulls we make, chances are we will nearly always lose our money. This is akin to a creative who is perpetually working in the desperate hope that simply plowing through in an always-on, nonrhythmic manner must eventually produce results. Certainly, some results will be generated—just like small jackpots that keep gamblers pumping coins into the machine—but over time this kind of activity only drains our creative bank account.

An investment mind-set, however, is focused on the long term. We know that we might not see an immediate return on our investment, but we know that we will see significant returns over time if we work the plan. When we build practices into our life that align with the underlying dynamics of the creative process, we will find that our overall capacity to create is growing. We will achieve long-term returns on our investment.

> **To spend our time effectively means that we are willing to view our time as a portfolio of investments, not as a slot machine.**

ESTABLISHING IDEA TIME

If you want to have a lot of great ideas, you need to structure formal time into your life to generate them. Sounds intuitive, right? Again, common sense is not common practice.

In every talk I give at conferences or companies, I ask the question, "How many of you would say that great ideas are critical to the future of your career or your business?" Without hesitation, nearly every hand in the room goes up. I immediately follow with the question, "How many of you had time on your personal calendar this week dedicated exclusively to generating ideas?" Crickets. Nothing. Maybe an occasional hand or two goes up.

Why the discrepancy? After all, if ideas are that important, why don't more of us spend time trying to generate them? I think there are a few reasons. First, many of us wouldn't know what to do with the time. We imagine hours spent staring at a blank piece of paper or standing in front of an empty whiteboard. Just the thought of it is enough to trigger the fight-or-flight instinct. Many of us don't do well in situations where there is a danger of feeling inadequate or unprepared; we'd rather do something we can at least check off of our to-do list than waste our time on something that might not help at all (or just make us feel stupid).

Second, I think that many of us have only experienced idea generation as a team sport. The only time we really spend trying to come up with new ideas is when we're in formal brainstorming sessions or staff meetings. Common practice in the workplace is that we generate ideas as a team, then go off to execute on our own. Sure, we may occasionally have individual flashes of insight as we plug away at our work, but we believe that kind of thing is accidental, a result of serendipity, and can't really be systemized. It either happens or it doesn't. Mostly, if we want to come up with ideas, we need to pull the team together and get out the flip pads.

While it's true that we can generate ideas effectively in a team context, to think that this is the only context for effective idea generation is simply false, and this is one of the skills that our company teaches. The fear of the unknown that prevents us from exploring creative problems on our own puts a cap on our creative output. While it's uncomfortable to think about wasting an hour thinking about the creative problems in our life and work, spending our time in this way can be infinitely more productive than filling that hour with e-mails and minor tasks.

> **No matter what you say about your priorities, where you spend money and your time will prove them out.**

As the old saying goes, if you want to know what's really important to you, take a look at your bank statement and your calendar. No matter what you say about your priorities, where you spend money and your time will prove them out. If you really believe that ideas are important to you, start putting your resources behind it. Begin by setting aside time for the sole purpose of generating ideas.

How much time? I recommend beginning with an hour a week. One hour, predictably scheduled, no exceptions and no violations. It's an appointment with yourself, a commitment to spend uninterrupted time on generating new ideas, not working on old ones. If you're like many creatives, you probably spend much of your week in execution mode. This time is not about execution or pragmatics; it is purely about new possibilities.

This is not time to strategize, write copy, design, or in any other way execute an idea you've already had. This is not time to do work; this is time to think about work. You are generating new ideas, not developing old ones. You are tilling the soil and planting seeds. While you may not always reap a harvest during these times, you are investing in future insights.

It's best to spend your hour of Idea Time working on one issue. I encourage clients to begin with their Big 3. Choose one of the items on your list and dedicate one uninterrupted hour focusing on generating ideas. How much could your work change if you made this a practice? How much could one idea change the trajectory of a current project?

I often face resistance from high-level managers or creative leaders when I suggest that they block off an hour per week to generate ideas. One fired back at me, "What?! You just want me to sit around and think?!" I reminded him that his company compensates him for the value he creates, not for the amount of time he spends in his e-mail program. I responded, "You can create an infinitely greater amount of value for the company in an hour of focused, skilled thought about critical problems than by responding to that e-mail slightly faster."

This may sound almost too obvious, even silly. "Put time on your calendar to generate ideas." It's so simple that it's tempting to dismiss it. But it's the small things that make you effective. It's your attention to details that sets you apart. Knowing does nothing for you—it's doing that matters. (Special thanks to Yoda and Mr. Miyagi for that valuable life lesson.) If you want to thrive you must dedicate yourself to doing the things that few people are willing to do. You need to go beyond hacks and quick fixes, and instead develop practices. Practices not only develop skills, they increase your capacity. They form the banks that allow the river to run deep.

When you begin to treat idea generation as a rhythmic practice, you begin to experience growth in your ability to generate ideas when you need them. Just like consistent repetition of any activity will give you mastery, you start to know what a good idea "smells" like. You build confidence in your creative ability and you do it in a low-pressure environment. (Who cares if you come up with terrible ideas? You're the only one who will see them!) These capacities are developed through patient repetition and regular practice.

GETTING STARTED WITH IDEA TIME

It's best to set aside time on the calendar when you are least likely to be interrupted. For years I have scheduled my Idea Time early in the week and early in the morning, before anyone else was in the office. This not only allows me to attack important creative problems before the stresses and logistics of the day have zapped my energy, it also starts my week off with new ideas that I can share with the team. (There's nothing more de-motivating than having an idea at 5 p.m. on Friday afternoon, then having to wait over the weekend to share it!) Your rhythms may vary, but the most important thing is to establish a time and stick with it.

If you don't think your manager will allow you to set aside time for generating ideas, you may need to make a case for why it's a good practice. Share the projects you're working on, the kinds of ideas you need to generate right now, and then show how you think this will benefit the organization. If you can show that the output of your Idea Time will ultimately make your manager look good, you're likely to get the go-ahead. If not, you can always plan time early in the morning or at the end of the day, or get permission to adjust your schedule to accommodate an hour a week of uninterrupted thinking.

What do you do in your Idea Time? The most critical thing is to begin with a clearly defined problem, preferably in the form of a question. (As we learned in chapter 4, about Focus, we call these Challenges.) Phrasing your problem as a question immediately gets your mind working on solutions rather than on the pragmatics associated with the project. For example, "Find new markets for XYZ" can easily be rephrased as "How can we expose more potential customers to XYZ?"

Once you've established the Challenge, use a large piece of paper or a whiteboard to record your ideas. (A few years ago I had a wall-size whiteboard installed in my office, as I was always running out of space to record thoughts!) A method that we've found especially helpful to process-oriented creatives is to surround it with a series of questions to stimulate new ways of seeing the problem.

Future. What would a solution to this problem look like? What would it feel like? What is the ultimate state that would describe that the problem has been solved? Write a few words, then start generating ideas off of them.

Past. What are some assumptions that are presently keeping us in gridlock around this problem? Are there any assumptions that need to be challenged or that could serve as a starting point for idea generation? Try to challenge one of these assumptions by generating ideas designed to disprove it.

Conceptual. What are other problems and corresponding solutions that I know of that are similar to this one? Are there any learnings from case studies or other items I've been exposed to that could apply to this problem? Try to force a connection between something you're familiar with and the problem you're currently working on.

Concrete. What are the specific and concrete attributes of the problem? Can the problem be broken down into three words? If so, do these words give me a new way of perceiving or attacking the problem? Free-associate new words off these concrete attributes and see if they spark any new ideas.

Take for example the Challenge "Make Commercial Air Travel Fun." (A tall order, no doubt.) The first thing to do is to make four columns on the page with the headers "Future," "Past," "Conceptual," and "Concrete." Then make a list under each header of words that immediately come to mind when considering the problem from that angle. In other words, free-associate— just write down whatever comes to mind.

Future (a few words indicating what a solution could look like): game, surprise, show, competition, entertainment, thrill, et cetera . . .

Past (a few assumptions about what air travel is like): challenging, boring, inconvenient, expensive, rude, uncomfortable, et cetera . . .

Conceptual (solutions to similar problems): cruise director, prizes, program director, Disney World ride lines, et cetera . . .

Concrete (specific attributes of the problem): delays, cramped, boring interior, bad food, et cetera . . .

Once you've written ten to twelve words per column, start choosing two words, each from a different column, and see if an idea is sparked. For example:

Cruise Director + Surprise = Have special celebrity "hosts" for random domestic flights.

Game + Prizes = Create a game for passengers in which they can compete for prizes.

Thrill + Boring Interior = Install a projection surface in the aisle of the plane, and a camera on the bottom exterior, then make the aisle look transparent to passengers by projecting a live image of what's underneath the plane at any given moment.

Write down everything that comes to mind, regardless of how impractical it seems. You'd be surprised at how many brilliant ideas are lurking just beyond your initial inhibitions. Often the first fifteen to twenty minutes of Idea Time will seem fruitless, but as you push through the temptation to check your e-mail or do something on your task list, you will find yourself gaining traction on the problem. It takes our minds a bit of time to adjust and focus on what we're really trying to do.

> **"The future is something which everyone reaches at the rate of 60 minutes an hour, whatever he does, whoever he is."**
> **—C. S. Lewis**

Because we so frequently field questions about what to do during these Idea Times, our team at Accidental Creative has developed a tool called the Personal Idea Pad (PIP) to help people generate ideas quickly and in a process-oriented way. It uses the Future/Past/Conceptual/Concrete framework to surround a Challenge and then free-associates concepts to find potentially useful ideas. We've found it very helpful for strategists, brand managers, and others who are more process oriented than more traditionally artistic types, though many designers and other more traditional creatives have said that it has provided them with a fresh way to tackle their problems. Additionally, we've found that having such a tool at the ready increases the effectiveness of Idea Time, especially as a starting point for new creative problems. (You can learn more about the Personal Idea Pad and purchase one at AccidentalCreative.com/book.)

As a warning: You will probably have regular Idea Times in which nothing of significance is generated. You will spend an hour spinning your wheels with little traction. This is OK. Remember that this is an investment, not something we're doing for a quick payoff. If you persist and continue the practice, you will also have times when you generate brilliant ideas in the first ten minutes—potentially business-changing ideas. Remember that tremendous value can be created in incredibly small amounts of time. You invest your time, focus, and energy in important problems, and you reap a return on the other side. It may take a while, but it's well worth it.

Jessie, a member of our online coaching community, AC Engage, said that prior to implementing Idea Time she struggled to maintain her energy level in her day job as an in-house graphic designer. She shared that the combination of establishing effective Challenges and Idea Time has been critical to her increased enthusiasm and performance. "I can't be on all the time, but giving myself small statements to focus on—like the Challenges—keeps my day on track. And I have found that I look forward to my Idea Time. I am excited to see what I can dig out of my own ideas after I get through the simple answers." We often see that increased enthusiasm is the result of clearing space to think about creative problems. Much of the angst and hesitation creatives feel toward their work is the result of fear and dissonance, which can be overcome with this structured thought time.

Make certain that you record all ideas that come out of your Idea Time, regardless of how irrelevant they may seem. Keep them in your notebook, or wherever you keep your notes, and review them often. Many times the best ideas for new projects are ones that were castoffs from other projects. If you make it a practice to value every idea by recording it, you'll be surprised how often you'll pull from these seemingly irrelevant ideas in the middle of a meeting on a completely different topic.

I frequently encourage teams to build this same Idea Time structure into their organizational rhythms. Getting the team together on a regular basis, perhaps once per month, to generate ideas around a nonurgent problem facing the organization is great practice for those times when there is a more urgent need for ideas. A sixty-minute session can yield ideas that carry over to other projects and become useful in alternative contexts.

Putting time on your calendar to generate ideas is worth it. It will change your life and your career. Remember: Successful, consistently brilliant people do the little (too obvious, too simple, too commonsensical) things that no one else is doing. This is what will set you apart, too.

PRACTICING WITH UNNECESSARY CREATING

In *The Artist's Way*, creativity expert Julia Cameron shares a practice she stumbled upon while living in New Mexico and recovering from yet another in a series of career disasters. Every morning, she writes out three pages, longhand, of pure stream of consciousness. In describing her method for "morning pages," Cameron says there is no need for editing or structuring the content. The entire purpose of the exercise is to get the brain moving and to circumvent any potential barriers to creative breakthroughs. "When people ask, 'Why do we write morning pages?' I joke, 'To get to the other side,'" she explains. "They think I am kidding, but I'm not. Morning pages do get us to the other side: the other side of our fear, of our negativity, of our moods. Above all they get us beyond our Censor."

What Cameron is advocating through the practice of morning pages is the act of Unnecessary Creating, creating for ourselves rather than for others. When we spend much of our time in on-demand creating, we can quickly lose touch with the passions that fuel our best work. We grow used to leveraging our abilities for the sole purpose of meeting others' expectations, and much of it is driven by hitting our marks rather than by exploring new possibilities. The ironic part is that this personal creative passion is the most critical thing we bring to the work we do. Creating on demand often causes us to lose the edge that fuels our best work and sometimes causes us to shrink from risk because of the potential consequences of failure.

When we create unnecessarily, we are setting our own agenda. We have permission to try new things, develop new skills, and make things solely for ourselves. If we fail, it's no big deal because we're the client. We can take as much or as little time as we need to get it right. The main purpose is to put our ideas into fixed form and to attempt things that we might not get to try in our day job. We can stretch ourselves, explore fringe ideas that intimidate us, and make things that no one but us will ever see. Without this practice in our life, we can become creatively stuck. We may experience a backup of ideas and thoughts, and the weight of all that we're not doing becomes a source of resentment and even guilt. We may feel like we're subverting our own life and passions for the sake of everyone else.

But who says this has to be the case? Your on-demand work is certainly a significant part of your life, but it cannot contain the sum of your creative effort. If you're looking for your on-demand work to be the expression of everything you have to offer, you will wind up very frustrated and go to your grave with your best ideas unrealized. The best way to prevent this is to carve time into your daily and weekly rhythms to work on the ideas that our on-demand role can't accommodate.

In his book *Shop Class as Soulcraft*, Matthew Crawford argues that there is a satisfaction to be gained from doing hands-on creating that can't be gained through more conceptual work. "The satisfactions of manifesting oneself concretely in the world through manual competence have been known to make a man quiet and easy," he writes. "They seem to relieve him of the felt need to offer chattering interpretations of himself to vindicate his worth. He can simply point: the building stands, the car now runs, the lights are on." Even though we don't always get to experience the satisfaction of completion in our on-demand role, Unnecessary Creating affords us this opportunity.

At this point some of us may be thinking, "I barely have the time and energy to do what's required of me for my job, and now you want me to take up a hobby?" It's tempting to resist this technique because we think it will add stress to our lives—yet another thing we have to cram into our schedule. But the experience of those who incorporate this practice is quite different. They find that it actually clarifies their thoughts, makes them more efficient, and reintroduces a level of passion for their on-demand creating. In addition, our Unnecessary Creating is often the best source of new insights for our on-demand creative work.

Robert, a creative director for a large brand-design firm, spent hours over the course of several weeks telling me about the stresses and pressures of his role. He told me that expectations were on the rise and that he had little authority to hire or shift organizational priorities to lessen the strain. He was stretched thin and had no room to breathe. I think he was expecting me to offer up some tips on time management, but to his surprise I asked him about his personal creating.

"What do you do for yourself?" I asked. "Do you create anything with your hands?"

He replied that it had been a very long time since he'd done much hands-on creating. Robert was at a point in his career where he was mostly directing others and rarely experiencing the satisfaction of actually doing the work. After a little more questioning, I discovered that Robert had once enjoyed painting with watercolors as a hobby, but it had been years since he'd had time to pick up a brush. As I probed further, I could sense his excitement building just talking about it. I challenged him to go to the store after work that day and pick up some watercolor materials. He agreed, and over the remainder of the week, I checked in a few times to see how things were going with his rediscovered hobby.

Over subsequent weeks, Robert and I would get together to talk about life and work, and I could see that there was a level of passion returning to our conversation. Engaging in something strictly for himself had unlocked a level of enthusiasm that had been subverted for years in the interest of practicality. Once he had permission to engage in something strictly for his own pleasure, he began to come alive, and I could tell that this was affecting not only his personal outlook but his creative engagement as well.

I've seen this happen with many others as well. Gardening, landscaping, writing, planning a side business, editing home movies, or anything else that provides an outlet for your passion and curiosity can be considered Unnecessary Creating. The main qualifications are that (1) the activity is something you really enjoy and (2) there is no time frame for completion of the work other than those you set.

GETTING STARTED WITH UNNECESSARY CREATING

As with Idea Time, Unnecessary Creating should have a set regular time for engaging in this creativity-inducing practice. Building this predictable infrastructure for your Unnecessary Creating will give you something to look forward to and will create a break in the middle of your hectic weekly rhythm. I'd recommend an hour per week as a starting place, but if you're really stretched, you can begin with an hour every other week.

One benefit of Unnecessary Creating is that it gives you the opportunity to regularly experience the phenomenon referred to as "flow." This is a term coined by researcher Mihaly Csikszentmihalyi to describe the sensation of "getting lost" in your work. One of the main contributors to flow is doing work that challenges your skills and requires your full creative capacity. When this happens, you lose all sense of time, becoming completely immersed in what you're doing. People who experience flow regularly report that they are able to access parts of their creative capacity that remain dormant during their less challenging work because they aren't required to take risks or stretch themselves.

Why is this important? Because this kind of stretching, skill-developing activity increases your capacity across the boards. You cannot separate your on-demand creating from your personal creating. When you develop skills during your Unnecessary Creating time, you gradually find those same skills and experiences being unleashed in your on-demand creating. You are exercising parts of your mind that may otherwise begin to atrophy. Unfortunately, the adage "use it or lose it" is an accurate admonishment for creatives. You need to make certain that you're not neglecting key passion areas or skills in your life just because your on-demand role doesn't regularly require you to use them.

> **"You have to leave the city of your comfort and go into the wilderness of your intuition. What you'll discover will be wonderful. What you'll discover is yourself."**
>
> **—Alan Alda**

HOURS

What should Unnecessary Creating time consist of? One technique is to keep all your potential projects in a Project Queue. Anything goes! Editing family movies, writing a short story or essay, rearranging your furniture, songwriting, developing a concept for a new business, or anything that requires you to exercise a degree of creative thought can count for your Unnecessary Creating. Keep a small whiteboard on your wall at home, and use it to track ideas for Unnecessary Creating projects you'd like to work on, or simply keep a list in your notebook or on your computer. Once you list the projects, you may want to simply attack them in sequential order during your Unnecessary Creating time. Some of these may be shorter projects, taking less than an hour, and some may be longer-term projects that require a week or more of your planned times. Regardless, it's best to work your way through the list so that you'll feel a sense of accomplishment as you check items off.

"Unnecessary Creating" is a misnomer; it's very necessary, indeed. Start small. Take notes on ideas you're excited about and things you'd like to do. Start a Project Queue. Set some time on your calendar. As you experience the benefits of Unnecessary Creating, you will be glad that it's a part of your rhythm.

Because so much of our time is spoken for by others, whether by your manager, your clients, or your peers, establishing practices that give you a sense of stability and provide a through-line is important and necessary. The practices discussed in this chapter are helpful in that they invest in your future capacity, fuel your creative process, and keep you from feeling like you're perpetually at the mercy of everyone else's agenda. By setting rails around your time and being purposeful about idea generation and skill development (through Unnecessary Creating), you are making an investment in future insights in your life and work.

The most common complaint I hear from creatives is "I just don't have the time." For 90 percent of us, this is an invalid excuse. I've worked with top executives with large families, men and women who sit on the boards of charities and who are very active in their community and are leading major work initiatives, yet they have still found the time to incorporate the capacity-increasing practices described in this chapter. It can—and must—be done. Time is available; you just need to find it. Most of us waste hours weekly that could be used effectively. The phrase "I don't have time" really means "There are things that are easier/less threatening/more comfortable that I'd rather spend my time on." If that's the case, I won't argue with you, but you need to be honest with yourself about the fact that doing your best work may not be a priority at this point in your life.

PUTTING IT ALL TOGETHER: THE CHECKPOINTS

9.

"Many have gone astray through not understanding how to continue a good beginning."
—Søren Kierkegaard

Remember that the objective of the methods described in this book is to establish a supporting infrastructure—a rhythm—that will provide stability and increased creative capacity. It will work only if you are diligent and consistent about incorporating the practices into your life. In order to do so effectively, you need to occasionally take a few steps back and think about your current needs.

The purpose of road signs is to keep drivers on the right course. If they appear too frequently, they simply become noise and are ignored. If they appear too infrequently, they are useless, because drivers are always unsure of whether they're headed in the right direction. In a similar way, you need to plan checkpoints at specific intervals in your life to ensure that you are still on the right course but not so frequently that so little has changed that you might be tempted to ignore them. These checkpoints help you establish and cultivate the practices discussed in this book in a way that they will facilitate meaningful engagement in your work.

Jeremy Pryor is the founding partner of the video production studio Epipheo, whose clients include Facebook, Google, and Yelp. He told me in an interview that with his very demanding schedule, he's had to learn to think of his life in terms of buckets, with regular analysis of what's on the horizon. This is the most effective way he's found to maintain sanity in the midst of chaos. He sets regular reviews of his rhythms, and whenever something seems awry in his life or work, his first question is "Is this a rhythm problem?"

To stay on course, this kind of rhythm analysis must be both long- and short-term. This is no different from what you probably already do in many areas of your life, though you may never have thought to apply this kind of strategic thinking to your creative process. A little bit of thought and planning time go a long way toward ensuring that you're not falling into the efficiency trap but are instead focusing on effectiveness.

Checkpoints slow you down, in a good way. Many creatives are aggressive in how they tackle their work, and they attack it with vigor. I have had to learn the hard way, many times in my life, to slow down. I like to move quickly. (I frequently run into automatic doors that don't open in time for me because I'm walking too fast.) I can sometimes get ahead of my team or my clients because I'm not stopping to make sure that we are all on the same page. Having occasional checkpoints in my schedule forces me to stop and reflect on where I'm headed and whether my life is really structured in a way that will get me there.

Checkpoints provide traction. Traction is gained when points of friction—even small ones—push off against one another and enable movement. Until there are two opposable surfaces, there will be no traction. Checkpoints act like strategic points of friction in your life to ensure that you're still moving forward and not losing traction. This will generate forward momentum in each of the five elements of Creative Rhythm and lessen the chance that they will get squeezed out of our life as the pressure escalates.

Checkpoints clarify opportunities. Think about how you've spent your last twenty-four hours. How much time did you spend on building something rather than on maintaining something that already existed? Many of us spend much of our personal and professional lives in obligation mode—we maintain a system that someone else invented, or simply maintain our relationships, reactively doing what we have to in order to get things done without building capacity for future work. These are symptoms of obligatory living.

A big factor in shifting from *obligation* mode to *opportunity* mode is thinking regularly about how you are investing in your capacity to do better work in the future and taking accountability for your own creative growth. To do so requires that you ask difficult questions at regular intervals and to have the courage to readjust your lifestyle as necessary to accommodate what's required of you in any given season.

You probably don't care about the pipes running through your walls (unless you're a plumber); you just want the water they deliver. Similarly, you need to be mindful enough of your practices only to ensure that they are present and functioning properly, but remember that they are there to serve you, not the other way around. Any system tends to become more and more cumbersome to maintain over time, and that's exactly what you must avoid. Simplicity is key. Simple rituals become habits, and good habits yield results.

Here are a few other critical notes about checkpoints:

There is no "one size fits all" solution for how the practices are implemented. The specific mix that works for one person may not work effectively for another, and you must be patient and willing to experiment. If you are diligent you will see results.

When the practices are implemented collectively, they work together like an engine with all of its parts intact. Your relationships impact your focus, which helps you determine what should be in your Stimulus Queue, and so on. When taken piecemeal, they still will provide improved clarity and insight, but you will not derive the full benefit that is present when all the practices are working together.

Get ready to compromise. Any degree of intentionality involves choice, and letting go of activities that have become comfortable and habitual may be awkward at first. In order to establish healthy habits, you need to let go of things that are making you efficient but not necessarily effective. This means that you may see a short-term dip in the amount of work you're producing while you are retraining your instincts about where to look for ideas.

There are additional materials, including worksheets, audio, video, and more, to help you engage in the checkpoints at AccidentalCreative.com/book. At bare minimum, for each Checkpoint you will need your notebook, your calendar, your work and personal project lists (if you keep them), your Stimulus Queue, and your Project Queue (of potential Unnecessary Creating projects).

WEEKLY CHECKPOINT

The Weekly Checkpoint is where many tactical decisions will be made regarding the practices. As your schedule is shaping up for the upcoming week, you'll have a much better sense of how and where the practices will fit most effectively into your life. I like to schedule my Weekly Checkpoint on Friday afternoon because it gives me a cliff-top perch from which to view my upcoming week and plot my course. Others I've worked with prefer to wait until first thing on Monday morning, or even to do this checkpoint over the weekend. If you have an organizational system that you're already comfortable with, you can also find ways of working your weekly checkpoint into your existing systems. For example, I've used David Allen's *Getting Things Done* methodology for years, and I like to lump my weekly checkpoint in with the weekly review suggested by David's system. Whatever works for you is fine, but be consistent.

During your Weekly Checkpoint you will think about how to implement the practices into your upcoming week. Here is a complete list of the practices we discussed in the book:

> **Focus:** Challenges, the Big 3, Clustering
> **Relationships:** Circles, Head-to-Heads, Core Team
> **Energy:** Whole-Life Planning, Pruning
> **Stimuli:** Study Plan, Notation, Purposeful Experience
> **Hours:** Idea Time, Unnecessary Creating

Block off twenty minutes on your schedule for the Checkpoint, then work through each of the practices and where appropriate schedule them in your calendar.

WEEKLY CHECKPOINT PROMPTS

> **Focus**
>
> *Challenges:* Look at, or create, a comprehensive list of your projects. Do each of them have associated Challenges? If not, create them.
>
> *Big 3:* What are your Big 3 for the week? Write Challenges for each of the Big 3.
>
> *continued*

Clustering: Are there ways you can structure similar work this week so that there is less task switching? Block specific time on your calendar for these activities.

Relationships

Circles: Do you have a circle meeting on the calendar? Do you need to prepare for it? If so, put time on your calendar.

Head-to-Heads: Do you have any head-to-heads this week? Do you need to prepare? When will you do it? Put time on your calendar.

Core Team: Do you need to reach out to a member of your core team for advice on something? If so, add it to your task list for the week or fire off a quick e-mail.

Energy

Whole-Life Planning: Are there any potential conflicts this week between work and personal activities or expectations? How will you get ahead of them?

Pruning: Is there anything that you'd planned but now realize may not be a good idea, given your upcoming schedule? How can you prune it? Additionally, are there any "hard runs" in which you'll have all-day or back-to-back meetings? How will you plan something energizing around or between them to prevent burnout and stay energized?

Stimuli

Study: When will your personal study times be this week? Put them on the calendar. What will they consist of? Take a look at your Stimulus Queue and map your week's stimuli.

Notation: Take just a few minutes to glance at your notes from the previous week as well as the indexes in the front of your notebook.

> *Purposeful Experience:* Do you have one on your calendar this week? When will it happen?
>
> **Hours**
>
> *Idea Time:* When will you structure your Idea Time this week? What will you focus on during these sessions? Put it on the calendar with the associated project name.
>
> *Unnecessary Creating:* What will you do for Unnecessary Creating this week? Put it on your calendar.

On page 188 is an example of what your week could look like after the Weekly Checkpoint.

You'll notice that all the practices are represented in this calendar, which will not always be the case. Each week will look different, but being purposeful about putting the practices onto your schedule before your time fills up will help you ensure that they don't get squeezed out. Additionally, you'll notice that the evenings are free and clear because this schedule demands getting out of bed early. Your schedule may be weighted more toward the evening if you tend to prefer being active then.

Also, depending on your preferences, you may want to combine exercise with your study time a few times per week by listening to audio books on the treadmill or while doing resistance training, or by going for a run while listening to a podcast or two. It doesn't really matter when the practices happen, as long as they are present.

Be sure to allow some space in your calendar to breathe. Don't be so rigid that you account for all your time, as unexpected interruptions are likely to interfere with your plans and frustrate your efforts. If you are coming into an especially busy season, you may need to ebb and flow with it, which is fine.

	MONDAY	TUESDAY	WEDNESDAY	THURSDAY	FRIDAY	SATURDAY	SUNDAY
6:00 a.m		Study (:60) *The Accidental Creative ch. 4–5*	Exercise/Study (:60) *Listen to 2 podcasts*		Study (:60) *Read Trend Report*		
7:00 a.m				Dentist (:90)		Exercise (:90)	
8:00 a.m	Review notes (:15)	Review notes (:15)	Review notes (:15)		Review notes (:15)		
9:00 a.m	Planning MTG (:90)	Conf. Call (:90)		Review notes (:15)		Take kids to park (2:00)	
10:00 a.m			Team Meeting (:60)				
11:00 a.m	Process e-mail (:30)						
12:00 p.m	CLUSTER/working lunch (:60) *invoicing*	Client Lunch (:90)	Lunch w/Joe for head-to-head (:60)	Lunch/Study (:60) *watch 2 TED Talks*	Lunch + call w/Jim from Core Team (:60)		Purposeful Experience (:90) *Go to museum*
1:00 p.m				Production Review (:90)	Client Review (2:00)	Clean garage (:90)	
2:00 p.m	Icea Time (:60) *XYZ Project*						
3:00 p.m						Unnecessary Creating (:60) *Novel story line*	
4:00 p.m	Process e-mail (:30)	Process e-mail (:30)	Process e-mail (:30)	Process e-mail (:30)	Weekly Checkpoint (:30) Process e-mail (:30)		
5:00 p.m	Buffer (:30) *bookstore*						
6:00 p.m	Family Dinner	Family Dinner	Family Dinner	Family Dinner		Family Dinner	Family Dinner
7:00 p.m					Dinner w/Russels		
8:00 p.m		Take a walk (:30)		Circle Meeting (:60)			
9:00 p.m							

MONTHLY CHECKPOINT

The one constant in the life of a creative is change, which means that you must regularly ensure that the plans you've made and the practices you've established are still relevant. The Monthly Checkpoint is about reviewing how the past month went, and recommitting to, or changing rails, around practices for the upcoming month. It's a way to gain a more clear perspective on your current priorities and workload.

The Monthly Checkpoint is an hour per month, preferably at the very end of a month (to plan for the upcoming one). The goal is to recognize trends in your work and to do some strategic thinking about which types of practices will help you most in the coming weeks.

MONTHLY CHECKPOINT PROMPTS

Focus

Challenges: What are the biggest projects you'll be working on in the coming month? Do each of them have Challenges? If not, create them.

Big 3: What are your Big 3 for the month? Write Challenges for each of the Big 3 if they don't already exist.

Clustering: As you examine the upcoming month, are there days or weeks where you can cluster project work in order to focus more deeply? If so, plan ahead by marking those days on your calendar.

Relationships

Circles: When will your circle meet this month? Put time on your calendar or send invites to members.

continued

Head-to-Heads: Do you have any head-to-heads this month? Put them on the calendar or send an invite to the other participants.

Core Team: Do you have any Checkpoints coming up with your core team members? You may want to schedule a lunch or a call. Send an invite or an e-mail.

Energy

Whole-Life Planning: As you survey the landscape of the upcoming month, are there any potential conflicts this week between work and personal activities or expectations? How will you get ahead of them?

Pruning: Look at your upcoming month; are there any especially busy weeks where you may need to prune either work or personal commitments in order to maintain a healthier energy level? Do it now, before things get too busy.

Stimuli

Study: Which items from your Stimulus Queue will you incorporate into your study times this month? Determine now what will best help you with your upcoming work and schedule. You may even want to create a note in your calendar on a weekly basis with the stimuli you hope to use that week.

Notation: Take a few minutes to review your idea index. Is there anything that may apply to upcoming projects? Is there anything that needs to be turned into a project? This is the time to do it.

Purposeful Experience: What kinds of experiences would you like to schedule into the upcoming month? What experiences would help you with your work? Create a list to use in your Weekly Checkpoints, or go ahead and put them on your calendar now.

Hours

Idea Time: Given the nature of your upcoming work, would your Idea Times be best placed at the beginning or end of your weeks? Which projects will definitely need some focused Idea Time? Make this list now to use in your Weekly Checkpoint.

Unnecessary Creating: What kinds of Unnecessary Creating projects will you work on this month? Take a look at your Project Queue and select the projects that seem the most appropriate given the time and energy you'll have this month. Add them to your calendar, or just make a list for use in your Weekly Checkpoint.

Additional Questions

In addition to the more practical questions about the practices, the Monthly Checkpoint is a good opportunity to ask some self-probing questions about your current work. While some of these questions may seem obvious or unnecessary, the answers can often be surprising.

How do you feel about the work you're doing right now? Do you feel like you're doing your best work? Why or why not?

What do you perceive to be lacking in your life and work right now? What can you do about it?

QUARTERLY CHECKPOINT

People are brilliant at developing permanent solutions to temporary problems. Though you may not often recognize it, you probably see this all the time in your organization. This is why we often see big, cumbersome bureaucracies within companies. Many of those bureaucratic systems were developed to deal with pressing problems at some point in the past and have now become energy-zapping dinosaurs. It also happens in our personal life. We develop habits to resolve problems, such as e-mail inundation, lack of energy, or a desire for relational connection, but then these habits live on once our needs have been met. The Checkpoints ensure that these personal bureaucracies don't take over your life and kill your best work.

Any of your practices can become more harmful than helpful if you don't adjust or prune them from season to season. This is the primary reason for the Quarterly Checkpoint. It is a check-in to help you evaluate how things are going and to establish the practices you think you will need in the next quarter in order to meet the demands of your life. It's like climbing a really tall tree to get your bearing and take a look at the upcoming terrain. It may seem like a temporary diversion, but this can make you much more effective as you continue your journey.

The Quarterly Checkpoint is the longest horizon planning you will do. While many productivity experts recommend annual retreats to examine goals and objectives, I find that these are often too long term to provide an accurate analysis of upcoming work. Ideally you will be able to take an entire day for this quarterly session, but, understandably, you may not be able to break away from your life in order to do so. If this is the case, the Quarterly Checkpoint can take place an hour at a time in the mornings or evenings over the course of a week.

One member of our coaching community shared how these Quarterly Checkpoints have been invaluable to her. She says, "They help to create balance in my life. I go to the library for about four hours on a Sunday afternoon armed with my daily notes and journal entries from the past quarter and my calendar for the upcoming quarter. I then analyze the past and plan for the future. It has been interesting stepping back from my own life and looking at it as an outsider. I look at where my energy has been going and where I want it to be going. I come away from the retreat with my Big 3 for the next quarter. The Big 3 go on my daily log that I use at my day job so I know what I'm really trying to do in life."

There are two main priorities for the Quarterly Checkpoint: establish your focus for the upcoming three months and set general rails around your practices.

QUARTERLY CHECKPOINT PROMPTS

Focus

Establish areas of focus. Divide a sheet of paper in two and on one side write "work" and on the other write "personal." Spend twenty to thirty minutes thinking of all of the commitments you will be accountable for. You want to be as comprehensive as possible because this will provide the working template for how you structure other elements of your plan.

A commitment is anything that you will be accountable for delivering. This can mean a large work initiative that will require a lot of creative effort, or it can mean a small personal project you're personally committing to get moving on. This is not a wish list of things you'd like to do someday; it's a list of things you are actually committing to doing or are accountable for doing in your work. If it's on the sheet, it's something you're planning to get done in the next three months (or planning to spend a significant amount of time working on).

What are the Big 3 for the quarter? These are the big conceptual hurdles you will need to jump this quarter in order to succeed in your work.

Establish Challenges for each of the Big 3. These should be phrased in the form of a question, and they should capture the

continued

main creative problem you need to solve. For each commitment you've listed, you should be able to answer the question "What am I *really* trying to do?"

Relationships

Once you have a sense of direction for the upcoming quarter and for the scope of your commitments, you can begin setting some rails for the other practices. Your relational rhythms are best examined on a quarterly basis to make sure that you are filling your schedule with stimulating interactions but not becoming overwhelmed with obligatory ones. Doing this will also help you determine where there are gaps in your existing relationships that you may want to fill in the upcoming season.

Who are the people you will be setting head-to-heads with this quarter? Have you thought through how this will happen? What is the best timing for your meetings? What kinds of things will you discuss? Take the opportunity afforded by your Quarterly Checkpoint to do an audit of all your relationships and to set new expectations around them. Perhaps you have standing meetings that need to be reevaluated. Maybe there's an old friend or colleague whom you'd like to spend more time with. Maybe there are some relationships that need to be put on temporary hold in order to account for the rhythms of the upcoming season. You have total permission to evaluate all your relationships with a clean conscience, then to make decisions strategically.

To some this may sound a little harsh. After all, how can we treat our relationships as a matter of convenience and discard them when they become cumbersome? To be clear: that's not at all what we're talking about. In fact, this is actually about making the relationships we choose to maintain more productive and meaningful. When we are selective about how and where we spend our relational energy, we find that our connections deepen and that we're actually able to give more of ourselves to the people in our life. It's when we're not selective that we end up living on the margin and giving leftovers to others.

Will you be meeting with a circle? If so, what will that rhythm look like for the upcoming quarter?

Think about your core team. When will you meet with them? You need to give these people enough notice so that they are able to give you their full attention when you meet.

Whom are you going to purposefully spend more time with this quarter? Are there people with whom you would like to spend more quality time in order to develop your relationships and possibly to gain mental traction on your work?

Energy

After you've listed each of your commitments for the upcoming quarter, you will begin to gain a sense of what you're expecting of yourself, or others are expecting of you, in the next few months. If you've never performed this exercise before, seeing the entire scope of your work laid out before you can be an eye-opening experience. It may even be a little overwhelming to see all your work and personal creative aspirations listed side by side. Not to worry—that's precisely the reason we're doing this exercise. A little discomfort now will save you a ton of stress down the road.

Each of these commitments represents not only time and creative work that you'll be accountable for but also energy that you'll be required to expend. As we discussed earlier, sometimes projects—even very good ones—can steal needed energy from more critical, productive projects. Many people don't realize the cumulative effect of their choices on their

continued

workflow. Ongoing, recurring creative commitments are often the result of a decision made once upon a time that continues to require energy and focus many months, even years, later. As these commitments begin to show up on your list, you see the true effect of choices you've made and how they may still be limiting your ability to engage with more pressing work.

Are there any projects that need to be pruned? Of all of the things on your list, is there anything that needs to go away this quarter so that you can focus your efforts on more productive work?

Is there anything else coming up this quarter that is abnormal but that needs to be considered? Are you taking vacation, or are there any other trips on the calendar? You need to take these into account, because they will affect your workflow and your energy. Often we don't look at how things like trips, time off, or family commitments will affect our ability to engage, and as much as possible, it's best not to plan our critical work around times when it will be difficult to mentally engage, like the last few days before a critical trip or the first few days back.

Remember that the purpose of looking at the scope of your commitments through the lens of Energy is to identify any easy decisions about what needs to be scaled back or where you may have unwittingly made long-term commitments that are becoming unwieldy.

Stimuli

What kinds of stimuli will help you with the projects you'll be working on? Can you identify any knowledge gaps in the commitments on your list? Are there any projects that will require special information? Now is the time to identify those needs and to list a few resources that may be able to help.

What are you curious about right now? List a few subjects that you're curious about or that you'd like to explore. If you can, list a few resources that are interesting to you and that you'd like to add to your Stimulus Queue.

How will you challenge yourself to grow? List a few items that you are going to study or experience this quarter as a way to grow your mind and stretch your experience base. These can be books, places you'll visit, meetings you'll attend, or anything else that causes you to see the world in a new way. The important thing is that you're listing concrete items and at least tacitly making a commitment to them.

Hours

Which of the projects on your list will require the most creative thought time? Can you identify four or five projects that will require an extra amount of creative effort? Not that you are going to do anything about it at this point, but it's good to begin identifying them now, in advance, so that you can earmark Idea Time against them.

What will your Unnecessary Creating projects be? Some of these may be listed already on your commitments list, but spend some time thinking about the kinds of projects you would like to initiate or continue this quarter. These items will be added to your Project Queue, and you will work on them during your Unnecessary Creating time. Again, it's not critical to get these exactly right. The whole purpose is simply to do an analysis of the kinds of things you're currently interested in working on and to make a commitment to trying new things and creating unnecessarily this quarter.

Dream a Bit

One additional exercise that has been effective for me is one I learned from my friend Lisa Johnson. She told me in an interview that once every several months she makes a list of all of the things that would "blow her mind" if they happened. For example, big business breakthroughs, people she'd like to meet or work with, or goals she'd like to reach. She relays that many of the items on these lists have actually happened, and she attributes this to the focus she gains from simply writing them down.

I've had a similar experience with this practice. I work it into my Quarterly Checkpoint and spend about thirty minutes dreaming as I write things that seem beyond my reach at the present. Numerous things I've put on the list have actually happened, such as starting my company, a family trip we wanted to take, and even publishing this book!

BEING INFLEXIBLY FLEXIBLE

Life will change and priorities will shift. This is the nature of creative work. As quickly as ideas are formed and put in motion, the entire playing field will often change and require new insights, new executions, and maybe even different team members to be added to our efforts. This is why the strategy of regularly reviewing your practices and asking whether they are truly aligned to your priorities is so important.

Some may be tempted to ignore this advice because it seems too obvious or irrelevant. I'd like to challenge you that life is too precious to allow for even a week of effort wasted due to being absent from the wheel. Once you get off course, a lot of energy and extra focus is required to bring you back to where you want to be. That's effort that could be used instead for projects you'd like to initiate or to generate insights you need for your work.

Once you've established deep patterns in your life around the practices, you'll likely notice that insights and ideas are emerging that you'd not expected. This is because you are no longer living reactively but are instead filling your life with more of what really matters to you and piques your interest. You are finding Creative Rhythm, and that is a great place to be.

COVER BANDS DON'T CHANGE THE WORLD

10.

"There can be an intense egoism in following everybody else. People are in a hurry to magnify themselves by imitating what is popular—and too lazy to think of anything better. Hurry ruins saints as well as artists. They want quick success and they are in such a haste to get it that they cannot take time to be true to themselves. And when the madness is upon them they argue that their very haste is a species of integrity."

—Thomas Merton, *New Seeds of Contemplation*

I'm hopeful that you've taken my encouragement throughout this book that the main reason to establish practices is to increase your capacity for insight and brilliance, not simply to cram more things into your life or to hack your creative process in some way. Again, there is no formula for effective creating and there are no shortcuts to experiencing brilliance when you need it. You will see results only when you are willing to let go of anxiety around short-term outcomes and pour yourself into activity that increases your capacity to experience future insights.

Over time, many of the practices in this book will become second nature. They will simply become intertwined with your lifestyle and creative process. But like anything else worthwhile, your first efforts will require a tremendous amount of forethought and follow-through. Once you've persisted in these choices, however, you will likely begin to see some welcome by-products in your life. Though it may take time to see these results, effective creating begins the moment you decide to reclaim the natural rhythms of your creative process and structure your life around them. This will require intentionality, choice, and discipline.

Intentionality means that you are approaching your life in a systematic way and not haphazardly. You know what you're about and you're working a system to make it happen. It means that you must constantly remind yourself of not only what you're doing, but why you're doing it (Checkpoints). You don't want your practices to turn into unhealthy, counterproductive habits or for the system to turn upon itself because you've disengaged from the why behind the what. This is like poison to your creative process.

Choice means that by saying yes to a set of practices, you are inherently saying no to a lot of other things. You can do almost anything you want, but not everything you want. What you choose to include in your life has consequences and immediately limits your other choices. Therefore, you must be careful when making commitments so as to not unintentionally limit your opportunities for engagement. Maybe you choose to create something or do a little reading instead of watching a sitcom. (Ooh . . . that hurts.) But you know that every choice you make affects everything else in your life, and you must therefore make these choices carefully. Choosing to establish study time, or Unnecessary Creating, or to set time for get-togethers with people who stimulate your creativity necessarily means you're saying no to other activities that may bring you more comfort in the moment. You are trading immediate gratification for future insights. It's an investment, and hopefully you're discovering that it's one worth making.

Remember: Comfort is frequently the enemy of greatness. When you choose to default to comfort, you are choosing to be less effective in your life.

Discipline involves establishing and hitting specific marks and doing what needs doing regardless of how you feel in the moment. It means that you make decisions when you have clarity and sufficient energy, then you follow through on them regardless of how you feel in the moment. It is human nature to default to the path of least resistance unless you make purposeful decisions to do what's best rather than what's most convenient. The time to decide to go on a diet is not when you're craving chocolate and the desert tray is waved in front of your face; it's when you're in a place of contentment and are able to rationally decide that you'd like to lose a few pounds. Similarly, the time to choose to study, or to build into relationships, is not when we realize you've come upon some unexpected free time; it's when you're strategically planning your life.

> **Comfort is frequently the enemy of greatness. When you choose to default to comfort, you are choosing to be less effective in your life.**

As you engage with intentionality, choice, and discipline, the capacities that have been lying dormant due to misuse or neglect become unlocked. You may uncover passions that you've long forgotten or remember how it feels to be fully immersed in your work and know that you're good at what you do. As these dormant parts of you come online, you will begin to see that your capacity to change the world is largely determined by your willingness to bring your unique abilities to the table every single day and to continually empty yourself of whatever's inside.

One of our coaching community members, Sal, shared how establishing practices and establishing Creative Rhythm unlocked new possibilities for him. He says, "I was going through changes and asking some important questions about who I am and how my work is supposed to reflect that. I was bouncing around between projects, tasks, and friendships, trying to figure out what I should be doing. Nothing was tied together. They were all individual and separate occurrences in time."

He continues: "For so many years, I had a wealth of creative talent built up inside of me. I would try to use a little bit here and there. Take a scoop off the top at work and apply it where I could. Try to start a new project to relieve some of the pressure building up. It was like I was drowning in a dull world and could only get a breath of creative oxygen every once in a while."

Sal says that once he became aware of how he'd been living without structure in his life, he began to establish practices that unlocked dormant parts of his abilities. He says, "Discontent is only a precursor for change and so it began. I began the process of starting a business. I wasn't sure what that business would ultimately look like, and I am sure I am not where I will end up, but the fact is, I started. When the time was right, I left my job and have been emptying myself each and every day since then."

Not everyone will leave their job, nor should they, but for Sal, establishing practices led him to realize that he'd been living his life by default and not with purpose. Once he'd discovered this, he began to align his life with his strengths rather than with what was most comfortable.

A LESSON FROM THE BEAVERS

A while ago, my family and I went to see an Omnimax movie about beavers. (Yes, we like to live on the dangerous side.) I've heard the phrase "busy as a beaver" at least a thousand times in my life, but I don't think I ever really connected with its meaning. Every day a beaver simply does what it's wired to do. It diligently performs the task of cutting down trees and moving them around to create dams. While the day-to-day work a beaver does may be relatively unnoticeable, over the course of its lifetime, a small family of beavers will affect the environment around it more than any other creature (except humans). Simply through the process of building dams, which it uses for housing and sustenance, a beaver can (and often does) turn a river into a meadow, or farmland into a lake.

Here's the thing: The beaver doesn't have some master strategy in mind for repurposing the surrounding terrain. This is not its intent. It is simply doing what it does, day after day after day, and the ensuing environmental change is simply a result of its activity. The beaver is just being a beaver, and it changes the very world around it.

So many of us want to go straight to results. We want to know how and when something is going to pay off from the very beginning. But how many of us, like the beaver, would be willing to work a little bit each day on something, all the while not knowing when and whether we will see the results of our labor? This is the benefit of having practices in our life. They provide an infrastructure to keep us focused on the things that matter most to our creative ability and ultimately they help us bring the best of who we are to what we do.

> "Your time is limited, so don't waste it living someone
> else's life. Don't be trapped by dogma—which is living
> with the results of other people's thinking."
> —Steve Jobs

I was recently speaking at a conference and stepped out with a few attendees for a quick lunch between sessions. As we left the restaurant to head back to the convention center, one of our lunchmates realized that he'd forgotten something at the table, so the rest of us waited for him on the corner in front of the restaurant. As we stood sharing smalltalk, our conversation was interrupted by a gentleman standing a few feet from us and leaning casually against a lamppost. He shouted, "What are you guys doing, standing around on the corner, holding a 'dirty shoe' convention?" We chuckled, acknowledged that we weren't, in fact, holding such a gathering, and went back to our conversation. A few seconds later, he interrupted us again, but this time his remarks were at another man passing by. "Hey! I thought that when the Romans fell, the sandals fell with them!" This quip also got a chuckle from us and caught the attention of the rest of the passersby as well. After a few more remarks about the footwear of people strolling by, the jokester retreated to a small shoeshine stand about twenty feet away, where he had a healthy line of patrons waiting.

Intrigued, I approached him to get a little more background on his story. It turns out that this was not a one-time gimmick but that he had been doing this for quite a while. He loves people, he loves humor, and had found a way to weave both into his daily routine as a shoe shiner. As a result of bringing his unique gifts and perspective to what he does, he'd built a loyal clientele and provided quite a bit of midday entertainment to random strangers. Rather than seeing his work as a set of tasks to be accomplished, he treated it as an opportunity to bring his own personality and passions to the world. The result is that he has built a one-of-a-kind shoeshine experience and earned a place in the hearts of countless passersby.

RECOVERING MEANING AND ENGAGING DEEPLY

One of the natural by-products of establishing rhythmic practices is that we begin to remember things that were once important to us that have somehow been forgotten in the hustle of our daily activity. Once we slip out of reactive mode and into a place of rhythm, space, and mastery of our process, we begin to understand that we have the ability to not only meet the basic objectives of our work but also to actually shape the work into something meaningful.

Whatever the subject matter of our work, as creatives we have the unique privilege of creating meaning each day. Whether we are designing a system, launching a new product, or consulting with a client, we bring something unique to the process that no one else can. With a bit of space and perspective, we will likely find that our work is less desperate and that we are drawing from a deeper well of focus, and perhaps even a refined sense of purpose. We begin to see how all of our life and work is interconnected when our daily activity is supported by our capacity-increasing practices. Our most significant work will nearly always come from a deep understanding of not only what we are doing, but the why behind it. When we gain a sense of mastery over how we engage our work, we are better able to connect with this deeper sense of motivation.

In a World Without Limits . . .

What would you do if you had all the time and all the resources in the world at your disposal? No limits, no constraints, no catches. You have complete and total freedom of time and movement. You can do anything, be anything, or go anywhere you want. What would you do?

For some of us, just thinking about this scenario gets our heart racing for a split second before we are pulled back to reality. We begin to rationalize and argue why this fantasy-world scenario is impractical and then our thoughts drift off to our task at hand or our e-mail. Some of us feel guilty for our fleeting excitement. We'll argue that it is impractical to even think about such things. At the heart of our very logical arguments is the reality that we don't know how to answer that question. We really have never thought about it. Our dreams, if we allow them, often seem highly practical and mostly centered around the prospective advancement, the next promotion, or something else in the foreseeable future. We are wed to the expectations of others or to a corporate culture that wants things from us—very practical things. (And rightly so, by the way. We are being paid for our time and the value we create.) But why is it that we allow others to define how we structure our life? Why is it that we refine and shape our life dreams based upon what's needed of us next quarter?

> **"The only true happiness comes from squandering ourselves for a purpose."**
>
> **—John Mason Brown**

Let me be clear: This has not been a book about achieving your life goals or finding your purpose. But as you begin to build structure and practice into your life, you will find that new possibilities open up to you. You begin to see opportunities that you previously overlooked. You begin to experience new ways of interfacing with the world as you regain a sense of ownership of your engagement. And the reality you find at the bottom of it all is this: you have something unique to offer and contribute to the world. But all of the time-management systems or strategic plans in the world will not help you get to work on it if you are not first willing to ask some difficult questions and then prune away all the things in your life that are getting in the way of it.

So many people I've encountered in my coaching and consulting have set the goal of working practically around the clock for several years in order to claim the prize of early retirement. Somehow they think that if they could only get all of this work stuff out of the way, then they could really enjoy themselves and do whatever they want—take up a hobby, write their novel, et cetera. They have so cast the dichotomy between work and play that they are incapable of seeing them as two sides of the same coin—as an expression of an engaged, focused, and passionate creative process.

I often hear "I'd really like someday to focus on helping orphans or the underprivileged," or "After this I'd love to spend time mentoring young designers," or other types of wishful thinking. But for now at least, these wishers feel like prisoners of this thing called "work" until the "great someday." They've divided themselves into two modes and assigned a purpose to each. One is for their "passions and interests," and one is for their "work."

OCCUPATION VERSUS VOCATION

> "What work I have done I have done because it has been play. . . . Cursed is the man who has found some other man's work and cannot lose it. When we talk about the great workers of the world we really mean the great players of the world. The fellows who groan and sweat under the weary load of toil that they bear never can hope to do anything great. How can they when their souls are in a ferment of revolt against the employment of their hands and brains? The product of slavery, intellectual or physical, can never be great."
>
> —Mark Twain

Because we tend to be possibility thinkers, many creatives spend quite a bit of time wishing for more alignment between our values, our passions, and the work that we do every day, or thinking about how we could better structure our work life as a platform for personal creative expression. Some of us believe that if we could only find the perfect job or work for the right company, many of our issues related to lack of fulfillment or occupational frustration would simply vanish. I've had this conversation, too many times to count, with creatives considering leaving their job to find something that's a better fit. While there's nothing wrong with seeking work that's fulfilling and that matches our personal skills and goals, often these conversations are less about the job itself and more about unrealistic expectations toward the employer or an overall lack of self-knowledge. Upon leaving their job, many workers find that they are right back in a place of dissatisfaction within a matter of months after taking a new one.

Why does this happen so frequently to the best and brightest among us? The problem is that many of us spend a lot of time thinking about what we want to do but little time thinking about who we really are and how to bring our full passion to what we do. We haven't learned to discern the difference between our occupation and our vocation.

Our occupation is how we make a living. In short, it's our job. It's what puts food on the table and keeps a roof over our head. It's the answer we give at a cocktail party when someone asks what we do. Hopefully, there are many parts of our occupation that bring us fulfillment and enjoyment, though there are likely parts of our work that are less than fulfilling.

Our vocation, on the other hand, is what we're inherently wired for. It's less likely to consist of a set of tasks and more likely to consist of a set of themes. For example, an accountant may technically describe his job by saying that he balances the books, but what really drew him to his job and continues to drive him to do great work is that he loves bringing a sense of order to the company's finances. It's likely that this drive to bring order plays out in areas of his life other than his job. Similarly, a manager may say that he strategizes, resources, and mobilizes his team, but the deeper theme that drives him is seeing people's potential unleashed. He is likely to seek out opportunities to unleash the potential of others through community service or mentoring programs, though he may not have thought much about why this is the case.

The word "vocation" comes from the Latin word *vocare*, which means "to call." As we each have a unique voice, we also each have a unique way of expressing ourselves through our work. It's the central theme that puts a fire in our gut when we encounter it or engage in work related to it. It's also the thing that fuels our passion, keeps us moving forward, and in some cases even obsesses us. Author Parker Palmer says in his book *Let Your Life Speak* that "from the beginning, our lives lay down clues to selfhood and vocation, though the clues may be hard to decode."

Once we do begin to decode them, however, our understanding of vocation will fuel our best creating. Having a grasp of how to apply our deeper passions to the work we do is the significant difference between doing work that's simply good and doing work that's brilliant.

Resonant Frequency

A few years ago I flew into LaGuardia on a red eye for an early morning meeting. Upon landing, I made my way to the restroom, where someone at the sink next to me made a comment about the flight delays we'd just experienced. I let loose a groan of acknowledgment, and upon doing so the entire restroom literally vibrated with my response. I'd accidentally hit upon the resonant frequency of the room. When I did, the acoustics of the room turned my tiny groan into something that sounded like a grizzly bear growl. My tiny effort was magnified significantly.

> Having a grasp of how to apply our deeper passions to the work we do is the significant difference between doing work that's simply good and doing work that's brilliant.

Similarly, when we do our work in a way that is aligned with our vocation, we often find that the tiniest effort on our part can have tremendous results. Our vocation is like the "resonant frequency" of our life. While we may never have thought about why, there are certain aspects of our life and work that just seem naturally energizing. By tapping into the resonant themes in these areas, we can unlock a whole realm of creative engagement that can be applied to the tasks we do each day.

I'll give you an example of how this has played out in my life. I've been engaged in a lot of different and seemingly unrelated projects over time, with Accidental Creative being the latest. A few years ago I sat down to analyze the common thread within all of them—my work as a creative director, my time in the music business, my work through Accidental Creative, starting a non-profit that funds international adoption, and others. As I spent time thinking deeply about the work that mattered most to me, I realized that the underlying theme in all these projects is freedom. It seems that when I really get excited about something, it's because I see the potential for others to find a new measure of freedom, whether it's that they're freed to do brilliant work (Accidental Creative) or freed from a cycle of generational poverty and placed into a family (our adoption-related work). Once I began to understand this as the core of my vocational work, my day-to-day tasks were illuminated, helping me to understand how I could better bring my best effort to the work I do. My best work, and my most creative work, is always fueled by this sense of bringing freedom.

Once I understood this, I began to formalize it. I dubbed myself the "arms dealer for the creative revolution," and I like to say that our company is "freedom fighting for the creative class." In this way, my work is defined by my vocation, not by the tasks I perform.

Question: **What are these deep points of resonance in your life? As you examine the times in your life when you've felt most engaged, most focused, and most brilliant, what are the common themes or connecting points?**

One helpful practice that we initiated on the Accidental Creative site was encouraging our visitors to write a "7 Word Bio."

This is a quick, seven-word statement that expresses the deep passion in their life or work. Some examples of 7 Word Bios on the site include the following:

"Help others see the ordinary as extraordinary."

"Using paint to capture amusing social interaction."

"A storytelling approach to life and work."

"Imaginatively blending structural elements into the land."

"Sharing my life stories, hoping you relate."

"Igniting people to thrive in their purpose."

Each of these bios serves as a kind of mission statement to guide daily activity. When I say that I'm "the arms dealer for the creative revolution," it means that I'm constantly looking for ways to equip creative people to do their best work by influencing their mind-set, giving them tools and helping them build relationships.

Challenge: **What's your 7 Word Bio? Share it with the world at AccidentalCreative.com/seven.**

DON'T BE A COVER BAND

Because we've understood the importance and effectiveness of bringing unique passions to the creative process, we've used the tagline "Cover bands don't change the world" for as long as Accidental Creative has existed. A cover band is a band that plays other people's music. The most extreme example is the tribute band, which directly copies another artist's music and style in the attempt to pay homage to their art. More subtle examples are the college rock bands that fill clubs every weekend playing the radio hits du jour. Occasionally you'll hear one of these bands rattle off something like "Now we're going to play something we wrote," and a collective protest arises from the clubgoers.

Why?

Because no one came to the band to hear the band's original music. They are there to dance, have a good time, and hear music they know. The promise of going to hear a cover band is that you'll be treated to familiar tunes in a dance-friendly format with little variation. This is the expectation. It's the "brand promise," if you will. When a cover band pulls an original tune from the repertoire, that promise is violated in a major way.

> **"Be yourself; everyone else is already taken."**
> **—Oscar Wilde**

It's incredibly difficult for a band to make the transition from cover band to one that plays original music. In fact, it rarely happens successfully. The band is always caught in the netherworld between making a living/earning money and wanting to express themselves through their art. Even if they are able to successfully slip some original music into the mix, they will always have to stare down the annoyingly vocal requests for the latest Top 40 fare or "Free Bird."

In my music business experience, the only way I've seen a band successfully earn a living playing original music is by choosing to do so from the very beginning and building a loyal audience for it. If they stay true to who they are and are willing to forgo the immediate financial return available to cover bands, they can sometimes build a long-lasting and loyal audience for their own music. However, they must be patient enough to earn fans, often one at a time. Choosing to chart an original path is not easy. As author André Gide wrote, "One does not discover new lands without consenting to lose sight of the shore for a very long time." This is not to imply that there's anything wrong with imitation. In fact, it's one of the critical phases of creative growth. We need to feel free to imitate others as we learn and develop our skills. But it gets tricky when we start making money based solely on our ability to imitate the creative work of others.

There are a lot of "cover bands" in the marketplace today. If their only goal is to make a lot of money, so be it. But the products and people who really change the game seem to be the ones who are able to stay true to a set of principles rather than being driven to quick returns. They develop a loyal audience rather than a fickle one that turns away the moment they play an original.

It's my desire to continue to strive to find my own voice and to try to weed out all the places where I'm being "cover-bandish." This can be a very tricky because it often means turning down more work than I accept, but my hope is that the original value that I bring to the clients I chose to work with will create raving "fans" who want to continue to work with me and trust me when I develop new products or ideas.

How about you? Are you willing to bravely pursue your own voice, carve your own niche in the marketplace and avoid the temptation to go for quick success? In looking at the long-term arc of your life and creating, are you willing to pour yourself into practices that will help you uncover hidden potential and unlock passions that have been buried beneath layers of expectations and obligations?

There is no greater reward than that of knowing that you are free from the need to be defined by pay or prestige, and are instead motivated by the very process of doing your work each day. This is how we begin to see the seeds of greatness spring up in our life.

HOW YOU DEFINE GREATNESS DEFINES YOU

How do you define "greatness"?

This is something that's been on my mind a lot lately, and it's something that I've been internally debating over the past few years. I spend a lot of time interacting with brilliant people and studying great minds, and the more I do, the more I've become convinced that how we define greatness ultimately defines our life.

If you define greatness as the pursuit of a bigger title and office, that will define your life.

If you define greatness as accumulating a lot of knowledge about something, that will define your life.

If you define greatness as being the best at performing some task, that will define your life.

If you define greatness as loving your family well, that will define your life.

If you define greatness as choosing to engage every single act and interaction in your life with purpose, that will define your life.

How we define greatness defines us. In the end, it's probably the single biggest determinant of the course of our life.

I once heard a South African friend share the reason behind the urgency with which he approaches his work. He said that many people believe that the most valuable land in the world is found in the oil fields of Saudi Arabia, the skyscraper-lined streets of Manhattan, or the diamond mines of South Africa. His contention, however, is that the most valuable land in the world is not in any of these places, but rather in the cemetery, because it is there that we find buried the unsurpassable value of businesses never started, novels never written, and dreams never pursued. He challenged listeners to "die empty."

This prompted me to write the words "die empty" on the inside of my notebook and to affix them to the walls at work and home. My goal, each and every day, is to get out of me whatever is inside that is of value to others. To do my work each day. To, hopefully, in some small measure, bring freedom to those with whom I work. As I do this, I am pursuing my own definition of greatness in my life.

In an interview for our podcast, brand expert Kristian Andersen said, "It's important to realize that you will be known for what you do, so you'd better get busy doing what you want to be known for." I couldn't agree more. Regardless of what this means to you, there is no better time than now to get moving on the things that are important, and that begins by choosing to establish rhythmic practices in your life and work.

I hope that you will join me in the effort to empty yourself each day, and to strive to find your unique voice. Don't go to the grave with your best work still inside of you. Die empty.

ACKNOWLEDGMENTS

This book is the culmination of many years of work and unending amounts of wisdom, support, and advice from heroes, friends, and colleagues. I am indebted in more ways than I can count. Rachel, thank you for your support and for bearing with my ideas. You are an amazing partner, and this book couldn't have happened without you. (I promise I will now stop talking about it.) To Ethan, Owen, and Ava, thank you for supporting Daddy's dream and for putting up with the times when I disappeared into my office to "write for a little while." (Yes, I'll read you a book now.) Thanks to Mike and Jane Henry for your support over the years, for helping me haul the upright piano to and from my first musical performances, for forgiving me when I caught the carpet on fire during that chemistry experiment in the third grade (or did I ever tell you about that?), and for giving me the space to explore my passions. To the McMullians and the Wertenbergs, thanks for your continued love, encouragement, and support of our family.

To my friends and advisers Jim Bechtold, Jerry Rushing, and Brian Tome, thanks for your advice and patient wisdom. riCardo Crespo, Peter Block, Ben Nicholson, Keith Crutcher, Steven Manuel, and Richard Westendorf, your continued friendship and inspiration fuels me, and I've learned so much from each of you. To my (brilliant) friend Lisa Johnson, I'm indebted to you for all your advice. I followed it to the letter.

To the "virtual mentors" who have greatly influenced my thinking and passion through their writing and work. Some are contemporaries and some not, but to each I am indebted. A short list includes Thomas Merton, Steven Pressfield, Seth Godin, Søren Kierkegaard, Parker Palmer, Peter

Drucker, Tom Peters, C. S. Lewis, Mihaly Csikszentmihalyi, and Abraham Joshua Heschel.

To the Accidental Creative team and those who have helped significantly in this effort, especially David Valentine, Matt Chandler, Joshua Johnson, and Lucas Cole, thanks for your support and brilliant work.

To my agent, Melissa Sarver, at the Elizabeth Kaplan Literary Agency, thanks for believing in me and for walking me patiently through this process. You are a gift, and you showed up at just the right time. Thanks also to Kimberly Palmer, who wrote the article for *U.S. News & World Report* that (eventually) opened these doors.

To my editor David Moldawer, Emily Angell, Amanda Pritzker, Maureen Cole, and the entire team at Portfolio / Penguin thanks so much for believing in this book and for your hard work at bringing it into being.

Thanks to everyone interviewed for the Accidental Creative podcast or for this book, including Seth Godin, Steven Pressfield, David Allen, Tony Schwartz, Chris Guillebeau, Lisa Johnson, Keith Ferrazzi, Scott Belsky, John Winsor, Stephen Nachmanovitch, Bryn Mooth, riCardo Crespo, Peter Block, Ben Nicholson, Richard Westendorf, Ann Calcara, Greg Hewitt, Simon Sinek, Gregg Fraley, Chris Brogan and Josh Kaufman.

To Burt Rosen, Steven Taylor, Blake Delanney, and the team at Le Meridien/Starwood Hotels, thanks for the opportunity to be a part of the LM100 Programme.

To the crew at the Madeira Starbucks, including Vanessa, Amy, and Melissa, thanks for hosting and fueling my 5:30 a.m. writing sessions.

To Mr. Bob Mowrey who first challenged me to think critically about problems.

To the thousands of creatives who are a part of the AC community, thanks for your encouragement, insight, and wisdom. I've learned so much from our interactions, and I look forward to many more in the years to come!

APPENDIX

▶ Tools to Help You Be Brilliant

Accidental Creative exists to help creatives and teams do brilliant work, and we've developed some tools to help you get the most out of your creative process. Below are a few mentioned in this book.

AC ENGAGE

Our virtual coaching community helps creatives and leaders apply the principles discussed in this book through regular audio and video coaching, online meet-ups and more. Learn more at AccidentalCreative.com/engage.

PERSONAL IDEA PAD (PIP)

This is a free-association tool designed to structure your creative thought, help you explore overlooked insights, and help you generate better ideas faster, whether on your own or with a team. Learn more at AccidentalCreative.com/pip.

IDEA TRACTION

This web-based software tool is designed to help teams meet less and create more by providing a virtual space for collaboration and idea generation. Keep all of your creative conversations in one place and share stimulus to spark new creative insights. Learn more or try it at IdeaTraction.com.

► **IDEA CULTURE TRAINING**

This immersive training teaches teams how to establish rhythms and practices that lead to a culture of everyday brilliance. Learn more at AccidentalCreative.com/ideas.

We have a variety of additional products to help you apply the practices you read about in this book. Learn more at AccidentalCreative.com/store.

► Resources Mentioned

Here are some resources mentioned in this book :

Making Ideas Happen: Overcoming the Obstacles Between Vision and Reality by Scott Belsky
> A helpful and practical analysis of why some creative teams are highly productive while others fail.

Creativity: Flow and the Psychology of Discovery and Invention by Mihaly Csikszentmihalyi
> Through brilliant research and interviews, Csikszentmihalyi explores the lives of successful creatives across a variety of domains and draws conclusions about why they succeed.

How The Mighty Fall: And Why Some Companies Never Give In by Jim Collins
> In this book, researcher and business expert Jim Collins explores common traits of companies that, though they seem unstoppable, eventually fail.

Linchpin: Are You Indispensable? by Seth Godin
> Godin challenges readers to find their unique space in the marketplace and to shun mediocrity.

The Now Habit: A Strategic Program for Overcoming Procrastination and Enjoying Guilt-Free Play by Neil A. Fiore
> From his own experience treating patients, Fiore shares how to overcome the factors that lead to procrastination and less-than-optimal work.

The Answer to How Is Yes: Acting on What Matters by Peter Block
> In this insightful book, Block shares how to act on what matters and by first getting the questions right.

Free Play: Improvisation in Life and Art by Stephen Nachmanovitch
  Musician Stephen Nachmanovitch shares the parallels he's discovered
  between musical improvisation and the art of living well.

Getting Things Done: The Art of Stress-Free Productivity by David Allen
  This highly practical book by Allen provides a step-by-step, fluff-free
  method for increasing personal productivity.

On Intelligence by Jeff Hawkins and Sandra Blakeslee
  A brain scientist and founder of Palm, Hawkins explains his theory of
  how the mind works and how we can leverage that understanding to
  build new technologies.

Amusing Ourselves to Death: Public Discourse in the Age of Show Business by
Neil Postman
  Though written in the 1980's, this book is prophetic and holds many
  lessons for those of us fractured by the age of the Internet and ubiquitous
  entertainment options.

Where Good Ideas Come From: The Natural History of Innovation by Steven
Johnson
  Johnson describes ideas as "networks" and shares how some of the
  greatest innovations of history came about.

*Who's Got Your Back: The Breakthrough Program to Build Deep, Trusting
Relationships That Create Success—and Won't Let You Fail* by Keith Ferrazzi
  A master networker, Ferrazzi shares insights into how to build
  relationships and develop deep connections with others.

A Whack on the Side of the Head: How You Can Be More Creative by Roger
von Oech
  Von Oech shares many highly practical ways to generate ideas when
  you need them.

*The Culture Code: An Ingenious Way to Understand Why People Around the
World Live and Buy as They Do* by Clotaire Rapaille
  A consultant to some of the biggest companies in the world, Rapaille
  shares how he uses cultural affinities and attributes to help companies
  develop new products.

Shop Class as Soulcraft: An Inquiry Into the Value of Work by Matthew B.
Crawford

Crawford shares his insights into why physical labor can be so fulfilling and why mind work can be dissatisfying.

How to Be Excellent at Anything by Tony Schwartz and Jean Gomes
This practical and research-driven book provides a deep dive into how to structure your life for maximal energy and effectiveness.

The Contrarian's Guide to Leadership by Steven B. Sample
Sample shares how some of the most effective leadership practices are those that go directly against the grain.

John Adams by David McCullough
McCullough provides insight into both the public and private life of one of America's founding fathers while also shedding light on how he approached his work and studies.

Birth of the Chaordic Age by Dee W. Hock
Hock shares some of his philosophy and how it led to his becoming one of the most successful entrepreneurs in the world.

Play: How it Shapes the Brain, Opens the Imagination, and Invigorates the Soul by Stuart Brown and Christopher Vaughan
In this fascinating book, Brown and Vaughan explore the curious connection between play, life, and work.

The Artist's Way by Julia Cameron
This engaging work by Cameron is a practical guide for reawakening the creative soul.

INDEX

product-versus-process tension, 38–42
Project Queues, 177–78, 184, 191, 197
project-review sessions, 41–42
project strategy, clarifying of,
    50–51, 63
pruning, 127–30, 132–34, 186, 190,
    192, 196, 208
Pryor, Jeremy, 182
purposeful experiences, 155–59,
    187, 190

quarterly checkpoints, 126–27, 132,
    191–97
    benefits of, 192–93
    dream lists in, 198
    prompts for, 193–97
    structuring study plans in, 143–47, 197

Rappaille, Clotaire, 107, 223
rationalizations, 103–4
ReachOut, 63
red-zone activities, identifying of,
    130–32
refining priorities, 70, 80, 85–88, 92
relationship-related practices, 21,
    97–112
    checkpoint prompts for, 186,
        189–90, 194–95
    circle meetings in, 98–104, 112, 186,
        189, 195
    core teams in, 107–11, 112, 186,
        190, 195
    head-to-head meetings in, 104–7,
        112, 186, 190, 194
relationships, 19, 21, 93–112, 122
    accountability cultivated in,
        102–4, 105
    benefits of, 94, 96, 98, 100, 109–10,
        111–12
    intimacy and generosity in, 96–97
    introverts and, 95
Republic (Plato), 145
resonant frequency, 211–13
retirement, 208
rhythmic practices and structure, 3,
    4–5, 20–22, 64–65, 69–217
    checkpoints in, see checkpoints
    in energy management, see energy
        management
    focus-related, see focus-related
        practices
    overall benefits of, 204, 205, 206–8
    personal definition of greatness and,
        215–17

recovering meaning and engaging
    deeply as by-products of, 206–9
relationship-related, see relationship-
    related practices
stimuli-related, see stimuli-related
    practices
three keys to implementing of,
    202–4
time-related, see time-related
    practices
varying results in implementation
    of, 6
rhythmic-versus-predictable
    tension, 34–38
ruts, creative, 34, 73, 115, 116,
    139, 140, 149

Sample, Steven B., 145, 224
Sawyer, Diane, 104–5
Schwartz, Tony, 4, 115, 119, 224
Senff, Tim, 63
serving others, 157
Seuss, Dr., 45
7 Word Bios, 212–13
Shop Class as Soulcraft (Crawford), 175,
    223–24
snapshot productivity, 36–37
specialization, 47
stimuli, 19–20, 22, 135–59
    characteristics of higher-quality,
        139–40
    creative ruts and, 139, 140
    potential benefits of, 139–41
    purposeful structuring diet of,
        142–47
    subconscious effect on mental
        processes of, 135–37
stimuli-related practices, 22, 141–59
    checkpoint prompts for, 186–87,
        190, 196–97
    converting information to creative
        insight in, 147–55, 157
    processing and notation in, 148–55,
        157, 173, 186, 190
    purposeful experiences and
        exploration in, 155–59,
        187, 190
    staying ahead of pressure with, 141
    study plans and cultivating in,
        141–47, 153, 186, 187,
        190, 197
Stimulus Queue, 146–47, 153,
    184, 186, 190, 197
Stone, Linda, 77